Unconditional

LOVE

Will Have You Serving Five Years Day for Day in a Maximum-Security Prison

QUINTIN FORD

PAGE PUBLISHING
Conneaut Lake, PA

First originally published by Page Publishing 2024

ISBN 979-8-89157-612-4 (pbk)
ISBN 979-8-89157-659-9 (digital)

Printed in the United States of America

It all started on February 11, 2012, three days before Valentine's Day. That was the first day that I met Tonya in person. Now we had talked on the phone. I met her on the chat line, so I really didn't know what to expect! I had talked to her on the phone all of January and the beginning of February, but I didn't see her face-to-face until February 11, 2012.

When I saw her for the first time, I could not stop smiling. She was beautiful, especially for her age. Tonya was forty-four years old at that time. I was twenty-four years old. Tonya did not look forty-four. She looked like she was thirty-four. She had a body that had a brother like, damn! Not only that, but she had a big booty with the thighs to go with it. She had some nice-sized breasts with a beautiful face!

The crazy thing about the day I met her was when she told me where she lived at—on Preston Street, which was right up the street from where I lived because I lived on Biddle in Green Mount. The crazy thing about that was I used to be all up on Preston Street, and I never ran into Tonya! We met up at the dome, which is right there off Preston and Madison Street.

She liked what she saw. She called me handsome! So I started smiling. It was a cold night that night, so I gave her a hug. Her perfume smelled so good. Behind the dome were some stairs where you can sit down, and so we talked for about an hour. She got cold, plus I had to work the next day, so I walked Tonya to her peoples where she was staying at. Her and her children lived with her cousin as well, so I walked her to the door where she was staying at. I gave her a hug. Before I could leave, she asked me for some money. Now this should have been a red flag—I just met you, and you are asking me for money?—but I paid it no mind. I gave her a hundred dollars.

She told me to call her when I got in the house. When I made it into the house, I called her and let her know, and I told her I would call her the next day when I got off work. I went to sleep. Tonya and I continued to talk on the phone as well as meet up at the dome. Now Tonya's daughter's birthday was February 26, so I met up with both at the dome, and I gave her daughter a hundred dollars for her birthday. Now we chilled for a while, but then I left because I had to work the next day.

The next day, Tonya called me and asked me if it would be possible to get her youngest son a pair of shoes, so I asked her what size of shoes he wore, and I also asked her to ask him what kind of shoes he wanted. He told her the shell toes which Adidas makes, so I bought him two pairs of shell toes. I called Tonya so I could drop the shoes off at the house, but she was not home. She was in class, so she said that her other son was in the house and that it was cool to give the shoes to him.

Now at that time, my daughter was three years old. Her name is Kiwi. She is my heartbeat. You never know the true meaning of love and unconditional love until you have children; my daughter is my everything now. Tonya, at that time, had five children—four sons and one daughter. Out of her five children, four were grown, and one was a teenager; the oldest was Keith. He was, at that time, twenty-five years old; yeah, I know he is older than I. He was Tree Top Piru. The second-oldest son was Jamal. He, at that time, was twenty-two years old, and he is gay. The third oldest is Chantelle, and she was twenty-one years old. She had a daughter named Mama, who, at that time, was two years old. The fourth oldest was Bryant. He was eighteen, and he was gone to the streets, and what I mean by "gone to the streets" is you could not tell him shit. He was popping oxycodone, drinking, smoking weed and cigarettes. He had no regard for anybody; he just did not give a fuck whether he lived or died. That's what I meant by "gone to the streets." Her youngest son was Damien. Damien, at that time, was fourteen. He is very smart and loved playing video games.

Now one of the ways I was able to provide for myself and my family was working for a subcontractor who had contracts for different warehouses such as Overflow and OST and more unloading trucks as well as loading up trucks. My homeboy Troy helped me get the job, and our boss's name was Pat. Now the job wages was not by the hour but by what you do, so for example, if I came to work and only unloaded a half of a truck, that's what I would get paid for. If I came to work and unloaded a whole truck, that's what I would get paid for. Now the pay on the trucks depends on what was in the container, so for example, if the truck was a twenty-footer and inside the truck were cases weighing fifty pounds each, that truck was worth forty dollars. Now when a forty-three footer would come in the warehouse and it had a 110-pound bags of black pepper, that truck would be worth ninety dollars.

Now when I would unload the trucks, I would unload the items onto a pallet. The cases would have to be stacked in block form. For example, there is a five-block six high, which means the first set of cases that will be placed on the pallet would be in five-block form, as well as the next stage of cases that would be placed on the pallet, but the stack of cases changes each layer. For example, the way the front cases stacked on the front of the pallet. On the next layer, the front becomes the back, and the back becomes the front. Each layer changes till you reach six high. When I was unloading the trucks, whatever the weather was for that day, it would be ten times worse inside the truck. For example, if it was 100 degrees outside, in the truck it would be between 130 and 150 degrees. Inside the truck was so hot to the point the inside of the trucks itself would be sweating! This job kept me in shape; I did not have to buy a gym membership to work out at all. All I had to do was go to work!

Now this was one of my incomes. I also received government assistance such as SSI, which stands for "supplemental security income;" I have been receiving SSI since I was eight years old because I was diagnosed with ADHD, which means "attention-deficit hyperactive disorder." I had anger issues as well, and I was receiving food stamps because my income fell into a low-income bracket. I also received $200 in food stamps, so my estimate net income, including the food stamps, was about $2,500 to $3,000 a month.

Now I just had moved back home with my grandmother because me and my baby mother went our separate ways. We used to fuss and fight back, then I used to have a lot of anger issues to the point I pushed her away. We grew apart from each other. We were living in an apartment together. She did not want to stay in the apartment anymore, and I did not want to stay there anymore either, so we both moved out and went our separate ways. We did not end on bad terms, and we both do co-parenting, taking care of our daughter. My daughter would stay with her mother, and I would get her on the weekends or when I was not working.

I moved back home with my grandmother, and she allowed me to rent a room. I was paying her $300 in cash and giving her $200 in food stamps. Now when I moved with my grandmother, my mother was staying there, both of my little brothers were staying there, and both of my cousins were staying there. Now this was a five-bedroom house with a basement. It was a three-story house with two bedrooms on the third floor and three bedrooms on the second floor, and on the first floor were the living room, dining room, and kitchen. My oldest cousin and his baby mother and his two sons were staying in the front room. In the second room on the third floor right across from my cousin room was my mother's room. My mother was staying in that room by herself, and you go down on the second floor, you have my grandmother's room. Then next to her room, you have both of my little brothers' room. They shared a room. Then you go farther down the hallway, you are going to run into the bathroom. Next to that was my little cousin's room.

When I first moved back to my grandmother's house, I was sleeping in my mother's room on the floor. We were living like black Mexicans packed in a house. That's one thing I can say about my grandmother. She always kept her doors open for everyone she loved. My grandmother had a big heart. I can say my grandmother always made a way for the whole family. She raised me and my other two cousins since we were babies. My mother was out there getting high off drugs, so my grandmother opened the door and took me in so I did not end up in a foster home. Now my mother is a phenomenal mother as well as a grandmother. It's just at that present time, she was at a bad place in her life.

My father, he was never around, never in the picture. It was to the point where if I would see my father in the street, I would walk right past him because I would not know who he was. The first time I saw my father, I was nineteen to twenty years old. He was not getting high or anything. He just was not in the picture. Even though my father was not in my life, he still taught me something very valuable in life, and that is what type of father not to be. I cannot make a baby and not be a part of that child's life. That would kill me. I would go to the ends of the earth to be part of my child's life no matter what. I was raised by the model, the definition of a real man is not who is the toughest or who goes the hardest, but I was taught the true definition of a man is the one who takes care of his responsibilities such as his family by providing for them, by protecting them by any means necessary even if it means sacrificing your wants and needs. Now that's the definition I was taught of a real man. Now even though I didn't have a father figure, I had two uncles who took me under their wing and taught me a lot of the dos, and in the don't, they taught me, "Anybody put their hands on you, better hit their ass back." They taught me not to take no shit from no one. When I was young, my uncles used to take me everywhere they went. My mother told me about the day she brought me home from the hospital and how she used to hold my uncle's drugs and shit, and when my uncle came into the room and asked her for the drugs; he did not notice me in the crib until she told him, "You are not going to say hello to your nephew?"

Uncle turned around to pick me up and gave me a hug. She said my uncle was a proud uncle ever since that day. Both of my uncles made sure I was good; my uncle's man used to beat my body to get a young brother tougher. My uncle Nookie used to rap to a young brother, and both of my uncles taught me how to get a female, what to say to her. My uncle's man showed me the street life, how to make money selling drugs. I remember going to my uncle man house when I got a little older. In every room, there was a gun tucked off somewhere. I remember he had an AK-47 in the trash can, as well as he had a machete in the house when my uncle went outside to sell his drugs. Furthermore, I saw him carry two handguns outside with him as well as a pillow with him. He put the two guns underneath the pillow, and he had his wife sit on the cushion while he sold his drugs. I said to myself, "Unc, that man was serious. That man was ready for war," and I will never forget what he told me one day. He said, "Nephew, I stay with a joint," which means a gun for those who don't know the street meaning. He said to me, "Nephew, I'd rather get caught with a gun than to get caught without it." He also said, "Nephew, I'd rather be judged by twelve than to be carried by six."

Both of my uncles gave me law at a young age, which means knowledge at a young age. They taught me right from wrong. I have sold every major drug there is to sell. I worked for my uncle. He showed me the game, the ropes. Even though I was exposed to the streets, that was not the lifestyle that I wanted. I loved to work a nine-to-five job. I loved working, getting a paycheck, and taking care of my family. I am not taking any shots at the brothers or sisters who are out there selling drugs. I am speaking on what I loved to do to provide for my family, and I say this to all my brothers and sisters out there, provide for your family the best way you know how. Whether you are selling drugs, selling clothing, whether you are working a nine-to-five get your money, take care of your loved ones. That's all that matters. As long as you and your family are happy and content with your hustle, I am happy for you. If you are a hustler, then hustle. Get your money.

Tonya wanted to get away for the weekend, so what I did was book a room at the Red Roof Inn out toward BWI airport. I asked Tonya what drinks she wanted as well as what food she wanted to eat now. Tonya loved to eat a lot of junk food, so she gave me a list of things she wanted. A lot of junk food like chips, chocolate cookies, chocolate cakes. All the junk food she used to eat went straight to her booty in her hips and thighs, so the list of junk food she asked me to get her included tortilla chips, the sour cream dip, as well as a chocolate bunny. She wanted Hershey with almonds as well as cook-ies. She wanted some Pepsi as well as some sunflower seeds. The list went on. It was a lot of junk food, to the point I had to put it all in a luggage bag, like I'd packed a bunch of clothes for a vacation. That's how much stuff was in the bag.

The day of the hotel stay, me and Tonya met up at the light rail. You should have seen me lugging around that bag. The bag had to weigh at least 120 pounds to 130 pounds, and I only had three things out of everything I brought. I'd gotten myself a bottle of Grey Goose as well as some chips and some condoms. The rest of it was Tonya's.

So we met up at the light rail, and we got on and rode to BWI Business Park Station. When me and Tonya got off the light rail, the shuttle came and picked us up. When we got to the hotel, I went in the building and picked up the key card to our room. Before we got to the hotel, Tonya asked me to get her a couple of muscles relaxers for her back from my mother, so when we got in the room, I asked Tonya what she wanted to eat. She wanted Domino's pizza, so I ordered the pizza. Tonya wanted some cheese bread. Before the food got there, Tonya had popped one of the muscles relaxers About the time the food arrived, she was feeling good. I got the food, paid for it, and then I went in the shower. When I got out, Tonya had eaten all the cheese bread. She had fallen asleep right next to the food as well. I started to laugh. Them muscle relaxers had her feeling good, so I started to watch TV.

About two hours later, Tonya woke up. She went and got in the shower, but before she did that, she asked me if I could get her some ice. "At the downstairs of the hotel, you can get ice," so I went in grabbed the ice. When I got back to the room, Tonya was still in the shower. Shortly after I got back to the room, Tonya came out the bathroom. She was wearing some sexy Victoria's Secret lingerie. Her skin was glowing, and she smelled good as a bitch. Her thighs and her booty were sitting out there I had a big smile on my face while trying to play it cool, trying not to seem pressed.

So she said, "Thank you" and smiled. I told her she was beautiful. She smiled once again, so I started putting ice in her cup. She wanted the Alize Red Passion on ice mixed with the E&J, so she had her drink in. I was drinking my Grey Goose straight, no chasers; you know how that Grey Goose had a brother feeling good. Tonya smelled so good. She had a red Victoria's Secret bra as well as

Victoria's Secret underwear, which was red as well. They fitting her booty like they were glued to her ass. That's how much they fit her booty. We both started to feel our drinks to the point we began to kiss and rub on each other.

I began to take my clothes off, and she began removing her bra as well as her underwear. We started kissing, then I started kissing and biting on her neck. She lay down on the bed and then I started eating her pussy while playing with her breasts. If only you could see her facial expression as I was eating her pussy, as well as hear the moaning she was doing, After I was done eating that pussy, she began to give me head. My toes started cracking. That's how good it was—my toes were curling. After she was done giving me head, I put on a condom and began to enter her pussy, which was wet as the ocean. Tonya's thighs and booty had me like damn, look at that booty. From behind she was fat as shit. I was hitting it from the back while grabbing her hips. Tonya had the type of booty that while I was hitting it from the back, her booty would bounce back. That booty sounded like hands were clapping, like a standing ovation as well as an earthquake. She got on top of me and started riding me. I was smacking and grabbing her booty. She was moaning pretty loudly as she rode my dick. She began to have an orgasm. She began to shake. She started calling out to Jesus as well. That Grey Goose had me going crazy, and that pussy. I was sweating bullets.

After me and Tonya were done, she went to sleep, and I had some pizza. I had worked up an appetite. Thirty minutes later, I was back in the pussy. So after the second time getting some of that good pussy, we both went and got in the shower. Then we both went to sleep.

The next day, I asked Tonya what she wanted for breakfast. It was a McDonald's down the street from the hotel. That was the only store that had breakfast, so I went and got me and Tonya some breakfast. When I got back to the hotel, Tonya was watching TV, so we both watched TV and ate our breakfast. We talked about life and family, then before you know it, we started kissing. Before I knew it, I was back swimming in that pussy.

After we're done having sex, we both went to sleep in. When we woke up, it was about 6:00 p.m., so we went and got in the shower. When we got out, Tonya wanted Chinese food. She wanted beef and broccoli with white rice. I ordered orange chicken and fried rice. Before the food got there, me and Tonya had gotten into an argument because one of her ex-boyfriend ended up calling her phone. I said, "I thought we were turning our phones off and enjoying each other?" She got upset about that, so she began to write in her journal. I heard a knock on the door. It was the food. I opened the door, and I paid for the food. I got the food and then I opened the bag and gave Tonya her food. It was the wrong food, so she got even madder. I asked her whether she wanted me to call them back, and I reached for her food. She said no, so I asked her if she wanted my food. She said no in an upset way, so for the rest of the night, we did not talk at all. I went to sleep.

To my surprise, the next day, Tonya woke me up to some head. I was asleep, and she was sucking my dick. Her head is the best, so she had my toes cracking early in the morning. That's how they were bending. After she was done, I got back into that pussy. She apologized to me while I was in the pussy. When we were done, I noticed that Tonya didn't have winter boots, and it was cold as shit outside. What I did was I got into the shower, and I got dressed. I told Tonya I would be back. I did not tell her where I was going. This was our checkout day of the hotel. We had to leave by 1:30 p.m., so what I did was I got the shuttle to the light rail and got on the light rail. I got off at Camden Yards. There was a Downtown Locker Room right there in the Gallery Mall, so I walked to the Gallery Mall.

I went into the Downtown Locker Room to grab Tonya a pair of UGG boots, and I grabbed me a pair of Jordans as well as my daughter a pair of Nike boots, a pair of Jordans, as well as a pair of UGGs. I went and got my daughter some outfits to go with her shoes.

When I got back to the hotel, it was like 1:00 p.m. Tonya had packed everything up, so I gave her the Downtown Locker Room bag and told her to open it. Her face lit up like it was a designer bag. She was so happy she gave me hugs and kisses. She said that what she needed was some boots. We checked out the hotel, and we got on the shuttle, and it took us to the light rail. We got on the light rail and got off downtown, and she called her son Jamal's homegirl to come pick us up from downtown. She came and got us in. She dropped me off at my grandmother's house, and she took Tonya home to her cousin's house.

So the day we checked out the hotel was a Sunday. I went and dropped my daughter's shoes off as well as her clothes at her mother's house, and I spent the rest of the day with my daughter because I had to work the next day. While I was chilling with my daughter, I got a text message from Tonya saying how much she had fun, how much she enjoyed herself. I told her I enjoyed being with her as well. Now Tonya had never met my daughter, so that Friday, I was spending daddy-daughter time when Tonya called my phone and asked if she could see me, so I told her yeah. This day was a little warm outside. Me and my daughter went and saw Tonya up at Johnson Square Elementary School. I introduced my daughter to Tonya, and Tonya reached out for a hug. Kiwi looked at her like who the hell was she. Tonya gave her a hug and was saying, "Pretty girl," Kiwi was looking like, "Daddy, why are you letting this woman who I do not know hold me?" That's how my baby girl's face was looking.

So we walked around to the playground part of the school. My daughter started playing while Tonya and I were talking. She was telling me about all the times she has been hurt by her ex. I assured to her that I would not hurt her, that I would not play games with her heart. I told her what she had in me as a man, that I would always be there for her through the good and the bad, that I would be there to wipe the tears from her eyes when she was crying, to be there for her when she was sad, to put a smile on her face and tell her everything is going to be okay, to be there for her to protect her from any harm that may come her way, as well as to be there for her to love her unconditionally. I told Tonya she had a ride-or-die man in me, and I told her I wanted the same in her. We both agreed that we wanted to be with each other.

At that time, I didn't feel like Tonya was serious about being together, so this was what I did. I got this test that I do, and it tells you what type of woman you are fucking with, and I know a lot of brothers who may have done this before starting off a relationship with their woman. I had my brother call Tonya's phone and tell her where he got her number from, so he called her. He told her he met her off the chat line, and he was trying to get to know her, She was like, "Okay," so I was like, "Bro, ask her if she is talking to anyone. Is she in a relationship?"

She told my brother no. I said, "Okay, bro, ask her if you can meet up with her and where she lives." She told him, so I told him to ask her what was a good day that they could link up. She told my brother the next day around about 6:00 or 7:00 p.m., so I told my brother, "Okay, good work." I appreciated it. Now what I should have done was have my brother meet up with her, and I would have been in the area and come out of nowhere and said, "This is how you keep it real? This is your word?"

So I called her and asked her if there was anything she wanted to tell me. She said no, so I asked her whether she had any plans for the next day. She said no once again. One thing I hate is a liar, especially when I am keeping it real and not giving you a reason to lie to me. She continued to lie, so I gave her the rundown on her plans for the next day, who she was meeting up with. I said to her, "That was my brother." She was so quiet. I couldn't see her facial expression, but by the way she was quiet, I assumed that her face had dropped into her lap, so I said, "I am being real with you, and I thought you were doing the same, but you are not," so she said, "Why would you do that? You set me up?"

I said, "You set yourself up. If you were a real woman, you would have said you were not ready for a relationship. You should have said you just wanted to be friends. Here it is, I thought we are in agreement with each other with wanting the same thing, but you are being dishonest. You are not loyal."

I said, "You can go ahead and go your way. I am going to go my way and find myself a woman that knows what she wants that's not a liar."

I told her to lose my number, and I hung up on her. All through that night, Tonya kept calling my phone; I ignored her phone calls.

She got her daughter to call my phone, and she said, "Q, that's not right. You set my mother up."

I said once again, "Your mother set herself up by trying to play a good man that is on her side. The problem with a particular woman who has been hurt by a brother that doesn't love them or care about them, they give that brother all the love in the world, and he just shit on all of their feelings, and that some woman will put up with as much bullshit with a brother who does not love her, who boldly disrespects her, and all of you will give that brother chance after chance, and he does the same thing every time, and some woman will lower their worth for someone who does not deserve them. And when a good man like me comes in the picture, I guess this is the time that woman gets her revenge by just shitting on a good man because she has been mistreated with disrespect and not appreciated by a man who never loved her, who never cared for her, but you know what they say about hurt people.

"So now God has put somebody in your life who genuinely cares about you and loves you, and you all still be having guards up from the last relationship to the point that some women do not realize that God has answered your prayers by sending you what you may have asked him for the whole time, which is a good man that is going to love you unconditionally, protect you, be there through the good and the bad, and who is going to love you the way you want to be loved, the way you deserved to be loved, like a queen."

Chantelle asked me to call her mother, and I told her that I didn't have anything to say to her mother. I did not want to hear what her mother had to say as well, and then I hung up the phone. Tonya continued to call, and I continued not to answer the phone. Now Tonya knew what block I lived on, but she didn't know what house I lived in because she had never been to my house, so about a week or two went by. Tonya came down the street to my block looking for me. Now I told you she didn't know precisely where I lived. She just knew what block I lived on, but she was determined to find where I lived, to the point where she went and knocked on one of my neighbor's doors. They told her exactly where I lived. I am glad it was not somebody trying to kill me because I would have been a dead brother thanks to my neighbors.

So she went and knocked on the door to my grandmother's house. My cousin Little Man opened the door. My cousin knows Tonya's daughter. He went to Dunbar Middle School with her, so when he opened the door and Tonya said, "Hello, is Q in there?" my cousin was like, "No, Q not in here," so her daughter Chantelle was like, "Yes, he is in there," so my cousin was like "No, he's not here." They started getting loud, so my cousin was like, "You heard what I said? What the fuck I got to lie for? Cuz not here!" He shut the door. Tonya and her daughter were waiting outside. Still the whole time, my cousin was telling the truth. If I'd been in the house and told my cousin to tell them I was not there, he would have, but I really was not in the house, so Chantelle went up the street to Tonya's cousin's house. Tonya stayed outside waiting to see if I was in the house.

I was across the street talking to Troy about work the next day, so when I was done talking to Troy, I left the house. To my surprise, I looked up the street and Tonya was standing on the corner. As soon as she saw me, she started walking down the street, so I said, "What do you want?"

She said, "What do you mean, 'what do I want'? That's fucked up how you set me up. That's very childish what you did," and I said, "You are just mad that a brother found out what type of woman you are." All the fuck she could say was I set her up.

I said, "I gave you that test to see if you were loyal and wanted the same thing as I wanted, which is to build something with you. The whole time you would have been doing you, I would have been faithful thinking you were doing the same, and you would have been cheating."

I said, "I caught you about to cheat. You just told me how you'd been hurt and that you did not want to go through that again. I gave you my word, and I said to you that I would not put you through that pain again. I told you that was my word, and here it is, you trying to hurt me. All I am trying to do is keep it real with you and build something real with you."

I said, "If you had got one of your homegirls or your sister to call my phone and do the same thing, here's how the phone call would have gone. Say her name was Ashley. She called my phone and was like, 'Hello, is this Q?' 'Yes, this is Q. Who is this?' 'This is Ashley. You gave me your number off the chat line.' I would have said, 'Okay, well, Ashley, I am sorry. I have a girlfriend now. I am currently in a relationship.' That's it and hang up the phone. That is it. No more than that."

We were arguing so loud that my grandmother sent my mother to the door to see if we were good as well as to call me and Tonya in the house. When we got into the house, Tonya spoke to everyone and had a seat.

On the couch, my grandmother said, "Are you all alright?"

We said yes. She told me and Tonya that our business was not everybody's business. Why were we out there yelling at the top of our lungs so everyone in the neighborhood could hear us?

Tonya said, "I am sorry, Ms. Rose." That was the first time Tonya had ever been to my grandmother's house. That was the first time she ever met my grandmother, so Tonya asked me if she could quietly talk to me outside.

I said yeah, so before we left the house, Tonya said, "Nice meeting everyone" as well as "See you later." We walked up to the dome area, and we sat down and talked about the situation that took place. She apologized. She was pleading for me to give her another chance to make the wrong that she had done right. She said she did not know if I was 100 percent all in with being with her, and she did not want to be the one to be hurt again. I told her I gave her my word that I would not play with her heart. "If this is not what I wanted, I would tell you than play games with you. I am not going to waste your time, and I want the same in return. If you do not want a relationship, then let me know right now, and you can go your way and I will go my way," so she said this was what she wanted, but is this what I want, given that she's twenty years older than me?

I said, "Tonya, if this was not what I wanted, I would not be up here talking to right now."

She said okay and asked for a kiss, so I gave her one. If only I had gone with my first instinct. I should have just walked away from the relationship with Tonya.

So Tonya and me started back talking and seeing each other. Her birthday was coming. It was the twenty-fourth of March, so I asked her what she wanted. She said a new phone. I got her a phone as well as a pair of Nike Air Max shoes that she did not know about, some cards with money in it, and some balloons. The day of her birthday, I had to work, so I told her I would see her that night. I called her on the phone, and she met me right there by Johnson Square Elementary School. She brought Jamal's godfather, Ronald. He walked her down the street, and I gave her all her stuff. She was so happy she had a big-ass smile on her face. She was very appreciative and grateful. This guy Ronald going to say I need a phone. I told him he need to go invest in one. She kept saying thank you and that she loved her gifts.

I said, "I am happy you love your gifts." I told her that I was about to go back in the house and that I would call her tomorrow when I got off work, so the next day, I went and got my daughter when I got off work, and we went out to eat. I brought her some toys as well as two pairs of Jordans. It was me and my baby girl's day. Later, I dropped my daughter back off at her mother's house because I had to work the next day. I went home and gave my grandmother and my mother some money. Tonya called my phone, and we talked for a little while, and then I told her I was going to sleep. I would call her tomorrow. We got off the phone at 9:00 p.m. My phone kept ringing and ringing. It was around about 12:00 a.m. I looked at my phone. It was Tonya calling. I said to myself, *What is going on?* She never called me this late, especially when she knew I got work the next day, so I called her back.

When she answered the phone, there was a bunch of yelling in the background. I said hello. She said, "Baby, I am coming down there before I kill this bitch." She told me her and Ronald had started to walk down the street to my grandmother's house.

I asked what the fuck happened to her. She told me her and her niece got into a fight. She said before she could say anything else, her niece punched her in the face, and they got to brawling. After, she said she was so upset to the point she blanked out, and when she came to, they were pulling her off her niece. Her sons and her cousins broke it up.

I said, "Just come down here," so I went downstairs and opened the door for her. We went upstairs. I gave her a washrag, a toothbrush, and a towel. She'd brought a change of clothes. I was tired, so I went to sleep. I had to get up at 6:00 a.m. in. It was already 1:00 a.m., but Tonya started watching TV.

I got up at 6:00 a.m., got in the shower, brushed my teeth, and got dressed for work. I kissed Tonya. I left the house and caught the bus to go to work. I called Tonya on a break after unloading one truck to make sure she was good and to see if she needed anything. She said no, she was good; my grandmother and my mother made sure she was good, so I told her I would be home in a little while. I called Tonya about 1:00 p.m. I got done around about 3:00 p.m. I did about three trucks that day. I made 150 that day, so I went home, and Tonya was still there.

She had gotten in the shower and changed her clothes. She was ready to go back up to her cousin's house, so I walked her up there. I made sure she got in the house and then I went back to the house. I got into the shower. I called my baby mother and made sure they were good as well. I talked to my daughter and told her I loved her and that when I got off work Friday, I was going to come pick her up. After I was done talking to my daughter and my baby mother, I went upstairs and talked to my mother and made sure she was good as well as my little brothers. I gave them some money as well.

Tonya called me while I was talking to my mother and brothers, so I answered to see if she was good. I asked her, and she said, yeah, everything was good. She wanted to meet up with me later during the day up at the dome, so I told her I would call her when I woke up.

I woke up around 8:00 p.m. I got up, washed my face, brushed my teeth, and I called Tonya and asked her if she was ready. She said yes, so I got dressed, then I left the house and started walking up the street. I saw a couple of my homeboys on our block. I said, "What up," to my homeys. Then I started walking to the dome. When I got there, I saw Tonya sitting on the stairs. She was looking good. She was wearing these jeans that were hugging, her booty, and her thighs, to the point you could see her underwear imprint, so I thought to myself, *Damn, she is thick*, and I was like, *I got to book another hotel so I can get some more of that good pussy.*

When she saw me, she started smiling, so I walked up and gave her a hug, and while I was hugging her, I grabbed her on her booty and started trying to palm all that, but it was impossible. She just had too much booty, so we sat down and started talking about the situation with her niece. She said they were not talking. She said they would pass by each other and wouldn't even look at each other. I said, "That shit crazy." She said no one even spoke to her niece because she was wrong for what she did.

I said, "You all beefing with her in the living in the same house with her. That shit is crazy."

Now I had bought the house up the street from my grandmother's house, which was at 620 East Biddle Street. My grandmother's homegirl told her that the woman that owned the house was tired of paying the ground taxes as well as the water bill even though the water was not on. Now the woman who owned the house was an older woman. She was like seventy years old, and her daughter used to live in the house. She had mental health issues. She would be talking to herself as if people were out to get her, so she would lock herself in the house and would not come out. Her mother and sister would bring her food and make sure she was good. One day they came to check up on her, and she was dead. After that, her mother didn't want the house no more, I guess because there was too many memories. Also, the fact that she found her child dead in the home where she raised her kids was too painful. No parent should ever have to go through the pain of burying their child. No parent ever wants to bury their children. It is genuinely a hurting feeling, someone you raised from an infant to an adult. I have a baby girl. I couldn't imagine burying her. Furthermore, I would be going in the ground with my daughter. I would not be able to live with that. It would kill me, so I can only imagine what she was going through. I was only able to talk to her once on the phone. She told me how much she wanted for the house and how she wanted to receive her money. My lawyer had written the contract up. I signed it, and her daughter brought her to my lawyer's office. She signed, so the agreement stated that she was selling the house for $1,700, and she was willing to accept her payments by installments of $200 every week. She wanted me to send the money through the mail to her address until all the money was paid in full. When the money was paid in full, she would sign the deed over to me. She had sent me the keys to the house, and I had gone in.

The place looked like a tornado ran through the whole house. There was trash everywhere, clothing everywhere to the point my legs were buried. There were bottles, paper, trash bags of trash. It was a three-story house, four bedrooms, one full bathroom, and a half bathroom downstairs on the first floor. Each of the rooms had a lot of trash and clothing. There was a bathroom on the second floor, and when you go upstairs, two bedrooms were up there. Now when you go to the bathroom on the second floor, that whole ceiling had fallen into the house to the point you can see outside from inside the house. You could look up and see the sky. There was a hole in the bathroom floor from where the roof had fallen in as well. The bathroom floor was not the only damage. When the bathroom roof fell inside the house, it had made a hole to the point where the studs to the bathroom roof traveled downstairs to the kitchen. It went even farther downstairs to the basement. Also with the roof falling into the house, when it rained, it would rain in the house. When it snowed, it did so in the house too, which caused the floors to be rotted, which means not only did I have to put a new roof on, but I also had to fix the floor so it could be a foundation so when the roof got put on, we'd have a sturdy base to fix it to so we don't fall through the floor. That was not all that needed to be fixed. When you go upstairs to the third floor to the back room, the window had fallen outside the house, so that whole wall had to be bricked back up as well. The window had to be reframed so another window could be placed back in there, but that's not just. For that room in the whole house, all the windows needed to be replaced. It was so cold in that house to the point where it was colder than outside. This house required a lot of work done to it, which meant it was going to cost a lot of money to fix the place up. What I told you were the significant things that had to be fixed. There was still a lot of minor things that had to be fixed with the house.

Now my homeboy Troy owned his house. He brought it as is. It was fixer-upper. He had put new electrical wires all through his home. He had to build new flooring. He was putting a lot of money into his house because when he brought his house, it was so fucked up. He paid one dollar for the home, so you can imagine how badly the house needed work, so I told Troy I was about to buy the house up the street from my grandmother's house. Troy asked me what needed to be fixed in the house. I said, "It needs a new roof in the bathroom, and one of the rooms on the third floor has to be fixed." I told him I had the keys to the house if he wanted to see the damages of the house I told Troy there was a lot of trash in that house as well. I took Troy and showed him the house.

When he saw the house, he said that the house would need a lot of work done. He gave me an estimate of how much I would have to pay to fix up the house extensively. The estimate that Troy gave me to repair the home was about twenty to thirty thousand. He said that I had to get rid of all that trash in the house. He said all I had to do was buy the black heavy-duty trash bags, and when the trash people came to pick up the garbage, just put two trash bags on his side of the street and put two trash bags on my side every trash week, which was every Thursday. Troy said he would help me get rid of all the trash. He asked me if he found any old movies or old magazines in there, if he could have them. I told him yeah, he could have that shit. I just wanted to get all that trash out of the house. He also said to me that if I got all the supplies to fix the roof in the bathroom as well as the sidewall in the room on the third floor, that he would help me fix them. Troy had some excellent advice. He said that I should work on one room at a time. He said every time I get paid from work, I should buy some supplies for that particular room, but little did I know, the city had other plans for that house.

Me and Troy, every day when we got off work, we would go up the house and bag up the trash. There was so much trash in each room that we had to use shovels to scoop it up and put it in the trash bags. It took me and Troy about four to five months to get all the trash out the house. During that time, Troy found some old movies and some old magazines. I found some old quarters that I gave to my grandmother as well as a painting that looked to be expensive, but looks could be deceiving. I did not have time to fix the house up. I would have had to go downtown to pull a permit in which an inspector would come out and check the house and give me a time frame on when all the work should be done. What I learned about the city is they are the biggest legitimate crooks you will come across. What I mean by that is that anybody that owns a house should know this: when you buy your home, you own the house but not the land that the house was built on, which means once a year, you have to pay ground taxes for the home you own being on the ground that the city owns. Now if you do not pay your ground taxes, the city gives you notice after notice. If you are still unable to pay your ground taxes, the city will seize your home, and it will go into foreclosure. This is one of the ways you can lose your home—if the city puts a fine on your house and you are unable to pay that fine. The city will give you time to pay the fine, and if you do not pay the fine in the time frame they gave you, the city will take your home. If you are unable to pay your water bill, the city can take your home. The best way to own your house is to buy the land as well because the price of the ground taxes, depending on the location of the property value, can be very expensive. Now little did I know at that time that the city had other plans for the house. The city got in contact with the woman who previously owned the house, and they told her that they wanted to buy the house. She said to them that she no longer owned the house. She gave them the number to the attorney who did the paperwork for me in buying the home. The city got in contact with my attorney and informed him that they were interested in purchasing the house, but I was not interested in selling the house. I planned to keep it and leave the home to my daughter. So they sent some forms to my grandmother's house, and the forms were basically income forms to see if I was able to fix up the place. Did I have the money to fix it up?

In the back of my house, the yard was not a fenced-in yard. It had a lot of grass and weeds that had grown and also had trash that people had thrown in, so the city inspectors came around and checked everybody's houses to see who was keeping up with their property and the ones whose property was not being taken care of, they would slap a fine on that house. The first fine may be $50 to $100, but if you do not fix the problem about time the inspector come back out to the house, then the subsequent fine the city slapped on your home would be $200 to $300. If you still ignore the payments, then the city will seize your house due to not paying your fines as well as not fixing the problem that caused you to get the penalty in the first place. The inspector pick times when they think people are not home. They show up when they think people are at work or just not home because you never see them. You just get a letter in the mail letting you know something on your property needs to be fixed or needs to be cleaned, and that's what happened to my house.

I got a letter in the mail stating that my yard needed to be cleaned. The fine was only $75, so me and Troy got all the trash out the yard, and we cut the grass. We bagged up all the trash and got it ready for trash day. Now I was going to fix the house and keep the home, but with the city wanting it done at a certain time or they would slap more fines, I told my attorney to see how much they were offering to buy the house, so my attorney took about two to three weeks to contact me. He told me that the city wanted to purchase the house for $6,700. The way they wanted to buy the home, they told my lawyer to tell me not to pay the water bill as well as any fines nor the ground taxes that they may put on the house. It's like they wanted it to go into foreclosure, but they still were paying for the house. So my lawyer informed me not to make no payments on the house. He said it would take a couple of months for all the paperwork to go through and for me to get my check. He told me that they would be mailing the money to his office, and he was charging me another $500 to do all the paperwork.

Now Tonya called my phone, and we talked. She asked me to come up to her house and chill with her. She was staying with her cousin now. I had never been to her cousin's house. I have walked her to her door, but I never actually went into the house, so I went up there. I am thinking that we were going to chill in her room. Hers was between the living room and the dining room. She had a single bed between the living room and the dining room, and her youngest son, Damien, slept in that bed. Right next to the bed, you got a little couch where her son Bryant slept at. Next to that, you have another little couch where Jamal slept. So I am looking like, "Are you serious?" She told me to sit next to her on the bed, so we got to talking.

The next thing I know, I am lying on the bed with my feet on the floor. She was lying on my chest, snoring, loud as shit, when I heard the door open. It was her son Bryant. Ten to twenty minutes later, I listened to the door. It was her son Jamal. Damien stayed at a family member's house. The whole time I was lying in that little-ass bed, a mouse was running across my feet like crazy. I woke Tonya up and told her I was leaving. She asked, "Why are you leaving?" I said I was going to get in my bed, that this shit uncomfortable. I told her I would call her tomorrow.

The next day after I got off work, I called Tonya and told her that I didn't know her in her children were living like that. I told her to start looking for a three- to four-bedroom house in which I am going to pay the first month's rent and the security deposit because they were living badly, so she started looking for places. Tonya called me. We were talking about the house that I owned, and she asked me if she could see the house, so she came down the street, and I took her into the house. We got to talking. Next thing I know, we were in the 69 position. I was eating her while she was sucking my dick. I said to myself, *Goddamn, what a way to break in the house.*

After we were finished, Tonya got up on me and started to ride my dick. She rode so much she worked up an appetite. We both bust a nut at the same time. When we were done, I walked her home, then I went in the house and got in the shower. After I got out, I called Tonya. She was in the shower, so she called me when she got out. She was devouring tuna fish. She'd really worked up an appetite, so me and Tonya started to plan another weekend getaway because my state taxes had come back, so I had that money, and also I had money from work. We were planning to go to the hotel downtown by the harbor. I was about to book the room when Tonya called my phone, and she was like, baby, could I do her a favor. I was like, "Baby, what do you need?" So she said that her housing came through, that the next day she had to look at the house. If she liked the place, then she would have to pay the security deposit and part of the rent. They would give her the keys to the house, and she could start moving in, so I asked her how much she needed. She said $277, so I took her the money so she could see the house if she wanted it. One thing about public housing, it goes by your income, but you will be living in the projects. That is why the rent is so cheap.

The next day, Tonya went and looked at the house and said she liked the place, and she gave them her security deposit. They gave her the keys to the house, so Tonya called me very excited. She said, "Thank you so much." Now she and her kids could move out of her cousin's house. She got her own shit now. I told her, "Congratulations, I am happy for you."

She said, "Now we do not have to go to the hotel." We could chill at her house. She said we could christen every room in the house before she moved in. You know I was down for that. Having sex in every room brought a smile to a young brother's face, so instead of booking a hotel, me and Tonya made plans to go up to her new house. I brought the drinks and the food she wanted, her E&J, I had got some Hennessy. She wanted Chinese food.

That same day that me and Tonya went up to her new house, I met her oldest son, Keith. We talked for a while, and he asked if I knew anyone who was selling any eight balls of cocaine, so I called my cousin Little Man to see if he knew anybody with eight balls. He said yeah, but he asked me if it was for me. I said, "No, it's for my girl's son." The brother he knew wanted $175. He was taxing, which meant an eight ball usually cost $125.

When it's a drought and no one has no drugs, a brother will raise the prices of their products because they know that the person who is trying to buy the product does not have too many options, and whether they were going to purchase the product or not, somebody would buy it, especially if it's a good product. This also sometimes happened when the product is good. The seller will raise his or her prices. Then my cousin adds another $25 for his troubles by him setting up the deal. He charged a fee. I told Keith the price. He was like, "Damn, that's too high."

I said, "I know," and I told him, "It's a drought in the city, so the price is going to increase." He said no, he was good. I would have said the same thing. That shit cost too much for one eight ball. Now this brother Keith, in the beginning, seemed like he was cool people. Later I would find out he was not cool.

So after Keith left the house, Tonya started to eat our dinner, then we began to drink our drinks. We put an air mattress in the dining room. Now this house was a big house. It had four bedrooms, two bathrooms, one full bathroom upstairs, and one half bath downstairs. It had a big living room and a nice-size dining room with a kitchen. The address was 716 Hope Street. The house was right behind the Save A Lot market, a nice little area in the projects. It was truly a laidback area.

After me and Tonya were done drinking, we started to kiss. I began to suck on her breast, then I started kissing and sucking and nibbling from her lips down to her pussy. I was feeling that Hennessy. I got to kissing and licking and sucking on her pussy for about an hour. She was moaning loudly as a motherfucker. She was having an orgasm. After I was done, I gave her a minute to get herself together because she was on another planet somewhere. After she came back, we started kissing, and I got up in that pussy. Now that pussy was so wet from her having an orgasm, it was dripping wet. That pussy was so good. While I am in the pussy, she began to shake and have convulsions I am thinking something was wrong with her, so I asked her if she was good. She said, "Don't stop, don't stop." She was coming again. I could feel that pussy getting even wetter. I was like, damn, that pussy so good that it was talking. It was saying, "Thank you, thank you very much." Now after about an hour and a half, me and Tonya were done. We got in the shower. Now she was just getting the keys to the house. She did not have time to get a shower curtain, so we took a shower without a shower curtain. We brought soap, wash clothes, towels, toothpaste, and toothbrushes. We took a weekend bag. After we washed each other up, we got out of the shower and dried each other off and got the water off the floor, then we went downstairs and went to sleep. I woke up the next day to Tonya calling me from upstairs, so I went upstairs to see what was up. When I got upstairs, she was ass naked.

She said, "Daddy, you ready to get back in your pussy?"

The room she was in was going to be her room, so we got to having sex. She was riding me, then I flipped her over on her back, and I started getting even deeper in that pussy to the point she began breathing real hard as well as moan even louder. Her facial expression said it all. Tonya was talking on the phone with one of her homegirls about the house, when she was moving in, so I came up from behind her and started to hold her from behind as well as grab her on her big booty. She began to smile, so she told her that she would call her back. When she got off the phone, we started to kiss. While we were kissing, I began to grab her booty, then I started kissing her on her neck as well as sucking on her neck, so we started having sex.

About two hours later, we were done. It took me a long time to nut like a motherfucker, so when we were done, Tonya was lying on my chest, and she said, "Baby, I want to thank you for everything you have done," and she told me how much she loved me. In the beginning, I wanted to believe that she loved, but she did not. I would later find out that the love Tonya said she had for me was not love at all. Now when I tell someone that I love them, there is no limitation on my love. What do I mean by that? There's not anything that I would not do for you. I will kill for you, I will die for you, I would go to jail for you. When I say "I love you," you got a person in me that's going to love you unconditionally. I will give my last to you. My love is genuine love and loyal love, and you will see that later in this book.

I should have gone with my first instincts with Tonya. I could feel the love was not real and that she was not for me. She did not love me for me. She loved me for what I could do for her, so she said how much she loved me and thanked God for putting me in her life. I was just listening and thinking, so Tonya started dozing off, and then I went to sleep myself. We woke up the next morning, got in the shower, brushed our teeth, and we got dressed. It was raining outside, so me and Tonya walked back over East Baltimore, which was not that far.

While we were walking, Troy called my phone and said there's work, mostly unloading trucks of 110-pound black pepper bags, so I said, "I will be there." I walked Tonya to her cousin's house, and I gave her a hug and a kiss, and I told her I loved her and went in the house, gave my grandmother a hug and a kiss on her cheek, then I went upstairs and gave my mother a hug and a kiss on her cheek and told her I love her also. My mother and I got to talking. She asked me what movie I wanted to watch. That's one thing about my mother—she had every movie you could think of. She had a store in her room with all the chips and candy you could think of, sodas, juices, cookies, and cakes as well. When me brothers and my cousins did not feel like going to the store, we go upstairs to my mother's room, and sometimes my mother would give deals like buy one, get one half off or buy one, get one free.

So my mother and I watched a movie. When the movie was over, I called my daughter and talked to her and told her how much I loved her and would be there to pick her up on Friday after I got off work. I told her good night, and after I hung up the phone, I got ready for work by hopping in the shower, brushing my teeth, and getting ready to go to bed. Before I went to bed, I played my little brother in a game of NBA 2K12.

So the following day, I got up 6:30 a.m. brushed my teeth, washed my face, got dressed for work. I left the house around about 7:10 a.m. I walked around the corner, passing the penitentiary. I walked farther down to go toward Dunbar football field in. Across from that football field was a senior citizen building. In it was a bus stop, and at that time, one of the buses that stopped right there was the 35 bus, which would carry me all the way up toward Sixty-Eighth Street toward Rosedale, and I would get off the bus and walk across and down the street to the warehouse. This day it was cold as shit outside. I love the wintertime even though I was born in the summer.

It was so cold outside too. You could blow smoke out your mouth, and you are not even smoking a cigarette.

The 110-pound bags of black pepper was only paying $90, so I unloaded the truck, about three in a half hour. The smell is bad, so what I always did was bring deodorant and cologne, as well as a washcloth with soap, and I would wash my chest and under my arms. A lot of the warehouses I worked at had bathrooms with sinks. They were not that clean, but it was clean enough to do a quick washup until I got home to take a shower. I would always carry a book bag with clothes and shoes and socks, with a washcloth and soap and cologne because I did not like getting on the bus smelling like sweat and whatever the truck that I unloaded was smelling like. I would make sure I stayed with my book bag to stay fresh.

After I was done with the quick washup, I left the warehouse and walked to the 35 bus stop. While I was walking to the bus, I called Tonya, and we talked about when she was moving to her house. She told me the beginning of April. I said, "That's my daughter's birthday month. My daughter was born April 14," so she asked me did I know what I was going to do for her birthday yet?

I said, "Yeah, we are going to go to Chuck E. Cheese. My daughter loved Chuck E. Cheese. "I am going to go pick up her two pairs of shoes, some outfits. I am going to take her to get her hair done." I said I was still thinking about what else I wanted to do for her birthday. First, I told her me and my daughter were going out for Easter as well."

We were still talking, and she said her son had gone over to the house and checked it out as well. They'd moved some of their stuff into their room already. She told me that she told her cousin that she was about to move. He'd told her congratulations, he was happy for her. She asked me if I would help her move, but she didn't have that much to move. Now the following week was the beginning of April, so she had a week to get her stuff packed, which was not that much. She said who was moving with her were her three sons, Jamal, Bryant, and Damien. She wanted to move in the house on a Tuesday, but what I didn't know was that Tonya had a lot of stuff in a storage unit that she was paying on every month, but the storage unit didn't have furniture. It was just boxes of clothes and boxes of paper. If you ask me, all the stuff in that storage unit was trash. It was paper of old mail, sales papers from the market, clothes that smelled mildew. The only thing in the storage unit that I would later find out that was worth keeping was the pictures of her family.

That Friday, I went in pick my daughter up from her mother's house, and we went out shopping we went to the Downtown Locker Room out in Mondawmin Mall. I brought her two pair of Jordans, then we went in brought her two outfits to go with her shoes. Now my daughter had an older sister and an older brother whose fathers at the time did not want to have anything to do with their kids. When me and Sharia were together, her kids became my kids, so before I had my own child, her kids were my kids, so even though me and Sharia had broken up, I would still take care of Kayla and Hayden, so when I would buy my daughter shoes and clothes, I would make sure I buy her brother and sister shoes as well. Hayden and Kayla needed some boots, so I brought them a pair of Nike boots. My daughter already had Nike boots, so I just got her two pairs of Jordan.

My daughter loved McDonald's for some reason. I don't know why. I think it's because the Happy Meals have toys in the bag, even when she had a million toys at home. She saw the McDonald's in the mall, and she said, "Daddy, I want to go the McDonald's."

I said, "Okay," so we went to McDonald's. I said, "Kiwi, what do you want to eat?" as if I did not already know what she wanted, so she told me, "A Happy Meal," so I told the woman who was taking our order. I ordered the Quarter Pounder meal. My daughter and I sat down and ate our food. I told her tomorrow, which was Saturday, I was going to take her to get her hair done. She said okay, so after we were done eating, me and my daughter went and got on the 21 bus stop, which would drop us off in front of my grandmother's house, so we got off the bus and went in the house. My mother and grandmother were sitting in the living room watching TV. Both of them were very excited to see Kiwi, and my mother yelled, "Kiwi, come and give your grandmother a hug and a kiss."

My daughter ran over there with a big smile on her face. Then she hugged my grandmother and kissed her, so after we were done talking, I ran my daughter a bubble bath and got her ready for bed. I knew I was going to have a hard day the next day because my daughter was blessed with a head full of hair when she was born; she got my hair because her mother's hair is long but nappy; my hair was not nappy. When you wet my daughter's hair, it would curl up. Now me and my daughter's hair is thick. My daughter has some good hair, but she didn't like getting her hair done, so every time someone does her hair, she gives them hell. I put my daughter in the bed, gave her a kiss, and told her I loved her and good night.

I went upstairs and talked to my mother. We watched a movie. I also gave my mother and little brother some money. I loved taking care of my family. I loved my family. I used to help my mother take care of my little brother Moses and my other brother Nathan. I was one year older than Nathan. I used to make sure he was good too. I love to provide for my family.

After me and my mother were done watching the movie, I went to bed so I could get up and get my daughter ready to get her hair done. The next day me and my daughter got up, and we brushed our teeth and washed our faces. We went downstairs to make her breakfast, some pancakes and eggs. She ate. I got her dressed, so she went upstairs with her grandmother and got on her nerves for a while until I got dressed so. After I was done getting dressed, I called my daughter, and we left.

When we got to the hair salon, the woman took my daughter's hair out and washed it; she blow-dried it and started braiding her hair down. My daughter's hair was long. It came down her back. She put all different-colored beads on her hair. I was surprised my daughter did not give her hell. I think it's because the woman was talking to her the whole time she was braiding her hair, so she took her attention off getting her hair done. After my daughter was done, we went and got something to eat. I told her how beautiful she was and how much Daddy loved her and don't let anyone tell her differently, so after me and my daughter were done eating, we went to the aquarium to watch the animals and then the dolphin show. My daughter was excited to see the dolphin show. After we were done with the aquarium, we went back home. My daughter was tired, so I got her ready for bed. I gave her a hug and a kiss and told her good night. I went upstairs to my mother's room. Both of my brothers were up there. They were watching a movie together, so when I got up there, the movie was going off, so we got to talking about me and Kiwi's day out.

My mother asked, "Did she cry when she was getting her hair done?"

I said, "No, she didn't cry. I think it's because the woman who was doing her hair took her attention off getting her hair done. She talked to her the whole time she was doing her hair, then after she was done doing Kiwi's hair, we went out eating. Then after we were done eating, I took her to the aquarium. She enjoyed watching the animals, especially the dolphins."

My mother said that it was good that Kiwi enjoyed herself. I told my mother I got to work on Monday. I asked her if she would be able to watch Kiwi until I got off work. She said she would watch her for me, so me and my mother got to talking about Tonya. She asked me when she was moving in her house. I said, "This coming Tuesday."

She asked if she was excited.

I said, "Yeah, her and her sons." She told me that I got a good heart. I said to her that I get it from her. One thing about me and my mother, we will give our last and not look for nothing in return, especially when we love you. I get that from my mother. She is straightforward. She doesn't bite her tongue. She is going to tell you what it is, especially when you are wrong. My mother's zodiac sign is a taurus. Need I say more? She doesn't take any shit, but that's my mother, and I love her with all my heart.

"So," she said, "Tonya seems likes she is cool. I am happy for you."

Next thing I know, my phone got to ringing. It was Tonya.

"What up, baby? How your day?"

She said, "Good, just getting ready for the move."

I said, "True that."

I told her me and my daughter had a daddy-daughter day. "I took her to get her hair done. We went out and ate and then we went to the aquarium."

She said, "Aww, that was nice. Did she have fun?"

I said, "Yeah, she enjoyed herself, especially when she went to the aquarium and saw the dolphins."

Tonya asked if she could see me tomorrow, which was Sunday. I said, "Yeah, we can meet up at Johnson Square Elementary School. I am going to bring my daughter too."

She said, "Okay, I want to see both of you all," so I said, "Okay, we will be there."

She said, "I love you, and I will see you all tomorrow."

I said, "I love you too. See you tomorrow."

After I got off the phone with Tonya, me and my mother were done talking. I played my brother in NBA 2K12, the one with Michael Jordan on the cover. We played a couple of games, then we played Call of Duty: Modern Warfare, so after me and my brother were done playing the game, I brushed my teeth, washed my face, and got ready for bed.

The next morning, me and my daughter woke up and brushed our teeth and washed our face. Then I fixed my daughter some breakfast. She ate her breakfast and then watched cartoons. I started washing clothes, getting ready for work tomorrow, so after I was done, I fixed my daughter lunch, tuna fish sandwich, and gave her some chips to eat with her sandwich. She had a juice as well. While my daughter was eating, I hung the clothes on the line so they could be dry and be ready for tomorrow. After I got done, I got Kiwi dressed and sent her upstairs to my mother's room until I got dressed. Later, I called my daughter downstairs. Before I left, I asked my mother and grandmother if they needed me to do anything or they needed anything before Kiwi and I left the house. My mother said no; my grandmother said she needed me to go to the store and get her some scratch-offs and her lottery tickets, so I said okay, I would go. I went to the 7-Eleven up the street and got her two five-dollar crosswords and two three-dollar crosswords, so after I got my grandmother scratch-offs and numbers, I went back to the house.

Two things about my grandmother is that she is a shopaholic as well as a "gambling-holic." She loves going to the market when they have sales going on. I don't care if the sale is out in the country, my grandmother is going to find a way there to get to them sales. I call her the notification alert woman because she is always telling me what market got the sales going on and how long the sale is going to last. My grandmother is also a gambling-holic because she used to stay at the casinos. She stays at the casinos to the point they would send her gifts, such as if she comes in to spend money at their casino, they will pay for her room for three nights as well as give her a free buffet. This was how I knew my grandmother was a gambler for real—when I saw the casinos started to give her money to come in gamble at their casinos; my grandmother spends about $200 to $300 a day on scratch-offs and lottery tickets, and you better not get her numbers wrong or bring back no wrong numbers. That goes the same for her scratch-offs. I done seen her curse people out because they brought her the wrong numbers or scratch-offs. Hell, I done been curse out for bringing her the wrong numbers as well as scratch-offs, so after I got my grandmother scratch-offs, I went back to the house and gave her the scratch-offs. She said thank you, so I told Kiwi to put her coat on and asked my grandmother if she was good. She said, "Everything is all right."

I said, "We will see you all when we get back," so Kiwi and I left. I called Tonya and told her to meet us at the dome. When we got there, Tonya was walking cross the street, so we met up at the same time. I gave her a hug and a kiss. She said, "Hello, li'l lady" to my daughter and gave her a hug. It was a bit warm outside. We walked down toward St. Francis High Academy School across from the high school. They had a playground; Tonya asked me who did my daughter's hair. I told her I took her to the hair salon, and they did her hair. My daughter ran to the sliding board and started to play.

Tonya said, "Your daughter looks just like you."

I said, "You have not seen my daughter's mother yet. She looks just like her mother."

She said, "No, she is your twin."

I said, "You see her mother, you will be saying she looks just like her mother. That's who her twin is," so she asked me if I had to work the next day.

I said, "Yes, I do."

She asked if I was still going to be able to help her move her stuff in the house. I said yes, I would be able to help her after I got off work Tuesday.

She told me her sons already moved their stuff in the house. She said they're all very happy that they had their own room and did not have to sleep in a living room.

"It was a blessing that your housing came through," I said. "God's time is always the right time."

She said she has been waiting on her housing for about four to five years."

I said, "Damn, you have been waiting a while."

She said, "Some people been waiting longer than that."

I said, "Damn, that's crazy. You go through a lot of these projects and see a lot of houses that are boarded up, with nobody living in them, and they got people waiting for years to call them for their housing. The city is fucked up. They be doing what they want. There's a lot of homeless people that have nowhere to go, and they got thousands of houses that they can put these people in that will get them off the streets because not every homeless person does not have a source of income. Some homeless people have an income but can only pay the rent. That's where housing can come charge them for rent utilities included with the rent that will get a lot of homeless people off the street, and for the ones who have no income, you allow them to stay there until they get an income. I just think the city could do a lot more for the homeless people. The city of Baltimore is overpopulated with homeless people. The people who run the government are so fucked up."

Tonya said she agreed with me. My daughter came over. Me and Tonya were sitting on the bench talking. My daughter said, "Daddy, can we go to the store and get some juice?"

I said, "Okay, Kiwi doodle." Down the street from the playground was a corner store, so me, my daughter, and Tonya went to the corner store. I told them to tell the store owner what they wanted because it was not one of them stores where you could walk in, grab what you wished to buy, and pay for it. It was one where you had to tell him what you wanted to buy, he would grab it and bag it up, you give him the money, and he gave you the stuff you brought. He had this bulletproof glass window that would keep him from getting robbed as well as shot at.

My daughter asked for her juice and some chips, and Tonya wanted a Pepsi, some chips, some candy, and a pack of Newport 100s. I got a Hawaiian Punch juice, so after we got our stuff, we went back to the playground. We sat and drank our juice and talked, so after me and Tonya were done talking, me and Kiwi walked her home and made sure she got in the house before me and Kiwi left. I gave Tonya a hug and a kiss and told her that I loved her. I would call her later.

My daughter and I started walking down the street toward my grandmother's house. When I opened the door, you could smell the fried chicken that my grandmother was cooking. It had the whole house lit up soon as we got in the house. My grandmother asked whether we were ready to eat. I said, "Yes, Ma," so my grandmother made me and Kiwi a plate. She had cooked fried chicken, fresh home-made greens and string beans, homemade macaroni, and cheese as well as a roll. Me and Kiwi gave God thanks for blessing us with the food. We also thank God for giving my grandmother the strength to prepare the meal. After me and Kiwi were done saying grace, we did not play with the food.

When we finished eating, the only thing that was left on the plate were the bones from the chicken my grandmother cooked. Everything was homemade; nothing she cooked came out of a can. She went to the market and got the vegetables, cleaned them, cooked them, and added her own seasoning to them. My grandmother said she started cooking when she was about ten years old. Her grand-mother from her mother's side told her how to cook. From upstairs, her grandmother would tell her what to put in the food as well as to what seasoning to put in the food. My grandmother said she would grab a stool, climbed up on it, and made sure her flames were low to the stove. She listened to her grandmother as she gave her instructions on how to prepare dinner. She was only ten years old cooking meals.

After we were done eating, I thanked my grandmother for the meal and gave her a hug and a kiss on the cheek. Kiwi said, "Thank you, Grandma," so after we were done eating, I put on cartoons for my daughter, and while she was watching cartoons, I played my little brother in a couple of games of NBA 2K12, then we played a couple of games of Call of Duty: Modern Warfare. After I was done playing the game with my little brother, I ran my daughter a bubble bath and got her ready for bed. I took her upstairs to my mother's room because I had to work the next day, and when I woke up to get ready for work, I did not want to wake up my daughter. So after my daughter was asleep, I went downstairs and got my work clothes ready for tomorrow. Then I got in the shower. After I got out of the shower, I brushed my teeth, then I went to sleep.

The following day, I woke up at 6:30 a.m., brushed my teeth, washed my face, and got dressed. I had to go to catch the 35 bus. I was going to the warehouse with Troy. We were unloading two black pepper trucks and a boxload of pineapples, so I went and caught the 35 bus to Sixty-Eighth Street.

After me and Troy were done unloading all three trucks, I called my mother and told her I would be home soon and how was Kiwi doing. She said she was good. I asked to let me speak to her.

I said, "Kiwi, what are you doing?"

She said, "Watching TV."

I said, "What are you watching on TV?"

She said, "I am watching cartoons."

I said okay. I told her I would be home soon. My daughter said, "Okay, Daddy. I love you. Be safe," so I started to laugh because of the way she said I love you, so I said, "Daddy loves you more, and I will see you when I get home. Love you." When I got off the phone, me and Troy walked to the 35 bus stop.

It was 4:00 p.m. now. The 35 bus always stays crowded, so crowded to the point it's packed all the way to the front of the bus damn near to the bus door. I expected the bus to be crowded today, but when the bus finally got there, it really was not that crowded. I was surprised. When I got home, it was about 5:30 p.m., so I went in the house, hopped into the shower, got dressed, and went upstairs. When I knocked on the door, my mother said, "Who is it?"

I said, "Your son."

My daughter heard my voice, and she broke her neck over to open the door. You would have thought she didn't see me in months the way she was acting, but that's real love. She was very happy to see me. When Sharia gave birth to our daughter, I knew she was going to be my heart, my everything. I knew it was not all about me no more. I had to think for two. Before, it was just me worrying about myself, planning for just myself, but after, when Sharia gave birth to our daughter, I had to plan for me and her. It was the day I learned about unconditional love.

So when Kiwi opened the door, she gave me a big big hug. She said, "Daddy, I miss you. I love you."

I said, "I love you too."

I said, "How was your day?"

She said, "Good."

I asked my mother how was. She said, "Good."

I said, "Okay, Kiwi, since you were good, we are going to the store."

She said, "Okay, I want a bag of chips and cookies and a juice."

I said, "Okay, get dressed," and so my mother got her dressed. We went to the store. I told Kiwi, "Get your chips and cookies and your juice," so she went and picked out all the stuff she wanted and gave it to me. I said, "That's all you want?"

She said, "Yes, thank you, Daddy."

I said, "You're welcome," and paid the store owner. I got our stuff, and I said, "Come on, let's go." She said okay, so we left the store. When we got outside the store, we ran into a couple of my homeboys, I said "what up" to my brothers. They said, "Q, your daughter looks just like you, bro."

I said, "Brother, you did not see her mother. She looks just like her mother, brother."

After I was done talking to my brothers, I told them I would holler at them later, gave everybody a five, and me and Kiwi walked down the street to the house and went in. Kiwi wanted me to put cartoons on for her, so she watched cartoons and ate her cookies. I started getting my clothes ready for work the next day. After I was done washing me and Kiwi's clothes, I called Kiwi's mother, and they started talking. Her mother was like, "Hey, Kiwi, I miss you and love you."

Kiwi said, "Miss you too, Mommy. I love you too."

I got the phone from Kiwi, and I started talking to her mother. I told her I would bring her home Saturday night. She said okay. I told her I would talk to her later, and I hung up the phone. Me and Kiwi went downstairs, and I fixed us something to eat. Tonya called my phone talking about the next day, which is her moving in her house. I told her that when I get off work, I would help her move her stuff, which was not a lot. She said her sons were excited about moving I said, "That's what up."

She said she told Bryant and Jamal that they were going to put something to the rent, that they were going to contribute in some type of way. She said they agreed to help her with the rent and keep her house clean. She said if not, they can stay there at her cousin's house, so everybody agreed to help their mother. I could hear in Tonya's voice that she was very excited about moving into her own house again. She was getting her independence back. Living in her cousin's living room with her kids, that can make you lose all sense of hope.

I was happy that I could bring a smile to her face. I am the type of man who always loves to help someone. I think that's one of the gifts God gave me. I get a joy out of helping, and I do not ever look for anything in return. I just love to help people if I can help them, I am good with that. I was just happy to bring some type of joy and a smile to Tonya's face and her children face because they had their own place.

So me and Tonya talked for a while, and she said, "Thank you again."

I said, "No problem. I am happy that I could help," so I told her I would call her the next day after I got off work. I told her I loved her and good night. After I hung up the phone with Tonya, I got my daughter ready for bed, and I took her upstairs to my mother's room. I went and got in the shower, and I went to sleep. I woke up the next day around 6:30 a.m. I got up, washed my face, brushed my teeth, got dressed, left the house, and got on the bus. We were unloading furniture trucks, which paid $100 a truck. We were unloading three trucks, so we made $150 apiece. I called Tonya and told her I would be at my house in about an hour and a half. She said okay, so me and Troy went and caught the bus.

When I got home, I went in the house and went upstairs and gave my daughter and my mother a hug and a kiss on the cheek and told them I loved them. Tonya called me and said she was going to leave her stuff in storage for another month or two, and she said she took her clothes and her younger son's clothes over the house in a ride, so I said okay.

She asked me if I would come over that night. I told her after I fed my daughter, gave her a bath, and put her to bed, I would come see her.

She said okay.

I said, "See you in a few hours." After I got off the phone with Tonya, I had daddy-daughter time with my daughter. I cherish every day that I spend with her. She is a little me. When you have kids, you see all the shit you used to do when you were their age. You can see how bad or sneaky you used to be. I always used to hear my grandmother say, "Wait till you get older and have children of your own. You're going to see all the shit you were doing because your child's going to give you all that bad shit back," and I can't lie, my daughter was bad as shit. It's like you get to relive your childhood through your kids, and you get to see all the simple and crazy thing you did as a child. So when my daughter did shit that's bad, I can't even be mad at her. I'd be laughing, and my mother would be like, "If that ain't your daughter..." She would say, "You couldn't deny her if you wanted to," and just laugh. I went in, fixed me and my daughter something to eat. After we ate our food, we colored in a coloring book. I read her a book, then we watched television. I can't lie. Being a father is one of the greatest blessings that God can bless anyone with. Nothing else in the world is more important than my daughter, and that's real talk.

After we were done watching her cartoons, it was getting close to bedtime, so I gave her a bath and got her ready for bed. I took her to my mother's room and put her to sleep. I talked to my mother for a while. I told her I appreciated her for watching Kiwi while I was at work. I told her I got her Friday when I get paid. She said, "Q, I don't watch my granddaughter for nothing in return."

I said, "I know, Ma, but I am still going to take care of you Friday because I really appreciate everything you do for me."

She said she loved me, and I said, "I love you more, Ma."

I talked to my little brothers. I told them Friday I got them too. I love taking care of my family. That's one of the qualities I got from my mother. She will give her last to her family; she would give her shirt off her back, and I am the same way, so after I was done talking to my brothers, I went and got in the shower, then I got dressed and went downstairs and made sure my grandmother was good. She said she was good and asked if I was coming back that night. I said, "Yeah, I got to work in the morning. Yes, I will be back." She said to be careful.

I said, "Okay, I will," and then I left out the house. Now the walk from my grandmother's house to Tonya's house was from East Baltimore to West Baltimore, but to me, it's like up the street because I was used to walking. Once you got past the light rail and walked, you were considered over West Baltimore. You got the unemployment building right there.

When I got to Tonya's house, I knocked on the door, and she opened her window and threw me the keys. I unlocked the door and went in the house. When I looked in the living room, they had the radio playing. Nobody was in the living room, and the lights were out, so I went upstairs. Everybody was in their rooms. When I got in Tonya's room, she had a pallet in the floor of sheets and quilts, and she had a night-light plugged in the wall. She had a radio plugged in that was playing slow jams, so I took my shoes off and lay right next to her, and we started talking. I was rubbing her back. She was telling me how her day was. She said her cousin was happy that she and her sons was gone. He said he would be over to check her house out, so she asked me how my day went. I said it was good. I told her I was thinking about her when I was unloading the truck.

She said, "What were you thinking about?"

I said, "Just chilling with you." She said she was thinking the same thing, and she laid her head on my chest with a smile on her face. She said she loved me and for me not to ever forget that I would later find out that when you see a person for who they are, never overlook it because that is who that person truly is. Sometimes the words "I love you" can be overrated because anybody can tell you that and not mean it, but if you show that person you love them, that speaks louder than you telling because we all know actions speak louder than words. I would later find out the love Tonya said she had for me was not genuine, so I said, "I love you too."

I told her I had to get up in the morning in got to go to work. She said okay.

I told her I would be over the next day, so I gave her a hug and a kiss and told her I love her.

She said, "Call me when you get in the house," so she walked downstairs with me in. She locked the door behind me, so when I got in the house, I texted her phone and told her I made it in the house in. I told her I would call her tomorrow after I got off work. She said okay and to have a good day at work. I said okay, so after I was done texting her, I went to sleep.

I got up the next day at 6:30 a.m., and I washed my face and brushed my teeth. I got dressed, then I went downstairs, said good morning to my grandmother, and made sure she was good. We talked for a minute, then I left to go catch the bus. When I got to the bus stop, the bus was coming up the street, so I was just on time.

When I got to work, we were unloading trucks with bags of Domino sugar that weighed fifty pounds per bag. I unloaded two trucks by myself, and Troy unloaded two trucks by himself. They were twenty-footer trucks, so after I finish my two trucks, I went over there and helped Troy finish up his truck. He only had four pallets left on the truck, so after we finished the rest, I called my mother and made sure she and my daughter were good. She said yes, they were good. I asked her if she needed anything from the store before I came home. She said she did not need anything from the store, so after we were done unloading the trucks, me and Troy went and caught the bus. While I was waiting on the bus, I called Tonya; she answered the phone. We got to talking. She asked me was I coming over there tonight.

I said, "Yeah, I am going to come through."

She said, "Okay, I am going to see you tonight." She said she loved me. I told her I loved her too. Now when I got home, I saw Kiwi downstairs in the living room, so when she saw it was me coming through the front door, she ran and gave me a big hug and a kiss on the cheek.

I said, "I love you, my Kiwi doodle."

My mother and my grandmother were downstairs. I gave both of them a hug and a kiss on the cheek, so after I was done talking to my mother and grandmother, I went upstairs and got in the shower. I got dressed and went and fixed me something to eat. My daughter had already eaten, so when I got done, I realized that the next day was Friday. I called Tonya and told her, "I am not going to make it over there tonight. I am going to spend the next two days with my daughter before I take her back home to her mother's house." I told her I would come see her Saturday after I took my daughter to her mother's house.

She said, "Okay, I love you."

I said, "Love you too. Talk to you later." After I hung up the phone with Tonya, me and my Kiwi doodle went to the playground, and she got on the swing, and I pushed her. She got on the sliding board. When she was done running around and playing, we went to the store, and she got her cookies, chips, and juice, then we went and sat on my grandmother's steps. She ate her cookies and chips and drank her juice. After, we went in the house and went upstairs to my mother's room and watched cartoons. Then I went and fixed her something to eat. I let her food digest and then I ran her a bubble bath and got her ready for bed.

I did not have to work the next day, so Pat came and drop off me and Troy's money, so I went outside and got my money. Troy was already over there at Pat's car getting his money. After, I went back into the house and gave my grandmother, my mother, and my brothers some money.

When Kiwi and I got up the next day, we went out to eat lunch before I took her to her mother's house. We ate our food, then we walked down the inner harbor then flagged down a cab. I took her to her mother's house. When we got to there, I told the cabdriver if he could wait, I wanted him to take me back into the city because my baby mother lived all the way out the Brooklyn projects out toward Curtis Bay, which is South Baltimore.

Me and Kiwi doodle got out the cab and knocked on the door. Her mother came to the door. I gave her all of Kiwi's shoes and clothes that I got her. She said, "Damn, you always buying her the new Jordan shoes. She still got new shoes in the closet she did not ever wear before."

I said, "Well, you could add these shoes to her wardrobe." She had shoes in the box that took up the whole top of the closet as well as the bottom floor. She had so many shoes to the point her mother was giving away brand-new shoes that my daughter could fit as well as shoes that she could no longer fit. She was giving away bags of brand-new shoes still in the boxes. I know what you all may be thinking, like that was ridiculous, but it wasn't. I will give my daughter my life. As long as I am alive, my daughter is not going to want for anything, and also when I was coming up, I used to always want the latest Jordans, but I know my grandmother could not afford the shoes, or at least that is what she told me even though she was getting a check for me by me having ADHD and anger issues. I know that was my grandmother's way to keep a roof over my head as well as put food on the table. My grandmother would go to the 29.99 dollar store and buy my shoes with the bit of money she had. That store was down on Broadway street. I never forgot that. My grandmother did not have much, but she did the best with what she had, so I always told myself when I was young that when I got a job, I was going to make sure I take care of my family, but I also said to myself all the shoes that I wanted but could not afford, I was going to buy them. All the clothes I wanted but could not afford, I was going to buy them, but not only that, I told myself if I were to have kids, my kids would have the newest shoes. I told myself when I have my kids, they would not have to go through that. I said I was going to work hard to give my kids the things that I did not have.

After I gave my daughter's mother her shoes and clothes to put in the house, I gave my daughter a big hug and a kiss on the cheek and told her I loved her. She went in the house. I told her mother I would call her later, and I went and got back into the cab.

When I got back to my grandmother's house, I called Tonya and made sure she was good. I told her I would be over there that night; she said she would be waiting for me. She said to bring her a pack of Newport 100, a Pepsi, and some chips. I told her I got her, so after I got off the phone with Tonya, I talked to my grandmother. I made sure she was good, then I went upstairs and made sure my mother and brothers were good. We got to talking about old memories. We were laughing and joking, so after I was done talking to my mother and brothers, I went downstairs to my room and got in the shower. When I got out, I got dressed to make my way over Tonya's house. Before I left the house, I made sure everybody was good. As I am walking from East to West Baltimore, I stopped at a 7-Eleven store and got the things Tonya asked me to get. When I made it toward the Wendy's that's over West Baltimore, you could hear gunshots ring out in one of the projects. I continued to make my way to Tonya's house.

When I was a block away, I called Tonya's phone and told her to come and unlock the door. So she told me that she's going to leave it unlocked for me. When I get to the house, the door was unlocked. I looked in, went upstairs. The first room at the top of the stairs was Damien's room. Across from Damien's room was Jamal's room. I could see that neither one of them was home. A little farther up was the bathroom, and next to that Bryant's room, so I went into Tonya's room. She was lying on the floor with some booty shorts on and a bra.

I said, "Damn, you are beautiful! Where is everybody at?"

She said Damien was at her sister Sony's house, and she didn't know where Bryant was. She said Jamal was over her cousin Glen's house, chilling with her niece. I sat down on the floor next to Tonya.

I said, "Tomorrow we are going to get you and Damien some mattresses from the furniture store. You all not going to keep sleeping on the floor." Now Bryant and Jamal already had beds Bryant sold drugs, and Jamal's godfather, Ronald helped in getting his new bed and his TV.

We got to talking and laughing and joking. To me, it was about more than sex. I loved this woman; I loved everything that came with her. I loved every day being around her. Not only that, I loved waking up to her in the morning, but I learned the hard way just because you love someone, that doesn't mean they love you or loved you at all. I learned a lot of people have ulterior motives for why they tell people they love them even though they don't love the person they are saying them three words to. That person may have money. That person may have a nice house or a nice car. Whatever the reason, maybe it's not genuine love. That's not me. If I love you, I love you to the end, and if I tell you I love you, there's not a thing that I would not do for you. There's a lot of people out there that like to play with these words and hurt a lot of genuine people that may really love that person. What I also learned is karma is a bitch because that same person that played with that three-letter word one day falls in love with a person that doesn't love them, and they end up playing them like that person that they played and told that they love them but really did not give a damn. We tend to mess over the ones that genuinely love us unconditionally for whatever reason. We may not be attracted to that person, or that person may not have any money. Whatever the reason may be, we will fall in love with a person that does not give a damn about us.

Me, I had to learn this the hard way, but now I really love a woman that's going to love me unconditionally because that love can withstand anything that this world throws at it. Continue to read this story to see how I had to learn about this firsthand. I learned firsthand you are only good to people when they need you or when they can use you to do something they know they cannot do themselves or would not do themselves. The minute that they do not need you or could not use you for anything, you can consider yourself useless to them, and they are on to the next person they can use, but some people really think that is love in this world.

So me and Tonya were lying there in the floor. She was lying on my chest. We started to kiss, and she began to take her bra and her booty shorts off. She lay down on her back with her legs wide open, and she started to bite her lips. I said to myself, *Damn, she is beautiful,* so I started kissing her from her lips all the way down to her pussy. I started eating her pussy. She began moaning quietly. As the minutes went by, she got louder. When I saw that she'd had her orgasm, I started sucking on her breast. She ended up getting on top of me and started to ride my dick. That pussy was so wet and good while she was riding me she began to talk dirty while looking me in my eyes and biting her lips. I began sucking on her breast while she was riding me. She started talking more shit. I started to smack her on her booty, then we changed positions. I got into that pussy from the back of her. Damn, she got a big-ass booty. That booty was clapping while I was hitting it from the back. I noticed the room begin to get hot, so I flipped her over on her back and began to get deeper in that pussy. I was sweating bullets. I know I lost a good five pounds. We were having sex, but it was like we were working out. Two hours later, we were done making love. I was hungry. Tonya was sleepy and hungry, so I ordered some Chinese food. Tonya went to sleep. When the food got there, I put Tonya's food in the refrigerator and ate some of my food, then I went to sleep next to Tonya. The next morning, me and Tonya got up and got in the shower together. We got washed up, got out the shower, and brushed our teeth. We got dressed to go get the beds for her and Damien.

So we left the house and caught the bus to the store called Discount Price Busters. They had reasonable prices on the furniture. Some of the stuff in the store is cheap. Some of the stuff is good quality. You just got to watch what you buy, so Tonya picked out the queen-size pillow-top bed with the rails to sit the bed on. She chose the full-size bed for her youngest son, Damien, with the rails. When we were done, I paid for everything. It cost about $400 plus taxes, which brought it up to $430, so they said they would deliver the beds on Monday because they were not open on Sunday. After I paid the money, I asked Tonya if she was hungry. She said yes.

I said, "What do you want to eat?"

She said, "Subway," so we went to Subway, so she ordered the tuna melt, and I ordered the cheese steak, so after we got our food, we hopped in a cab and went to her house. We listened to the music while we ate our food. When we were done eating, we walked up the street to Pennsylvania Avenue. It was a Family Dollar up there. I brought her all her household things—bleach, mops, brooms, buckets, trash cans. I brought everything you would need when you just moved in a house as far as cleaning supplies. When she was done, I think the price was about $175. After I paid for everything, I waved down a hack to drive us down the street. I paid $10 for bringing me and Tonya down the street to her house. I brought all the bags in the house, and Tonya put everything where she wanted the things.

Bryant was upstairs in his room. He was playing music. Now Bryant and his mother really didn't get along. He probably felt like his mother really didn't care about him. She felt that he was disrespectful. He had stolen money from her as well as family members. She told me about the time he broke into his grandmother and grandfather's house, who are Christians, so each one of them had some type of resentment to each other. He probably felt like his mother putting him away so many times that she really didn't care. He was in group home after group home, in a juvenile detention center, as well as locked up. He snapped out in jail to the point three COs beat him. They knocked his two front teeth out. Things like that can leave you with resentment in your heart. Shit like that can make your heart cold to any and everyone including your family. That's one of the reasons Bryant and his mother had their problems. She was telling me how she really didn't want him to move with her because she knew that he, out of her other children, would cause the most problem. Come to find out she would be right.

Bryant came downstairs and asked his mother for a cigarette. She gave him one. He lit the cigarette on the stove and then went back upstairs. Tonya got to making mop water. She was about to mop the kitchen and the dining room as well as the bathroom downstairs in the hallway. While she was cleaning, I went upstairs and called to check up on my daughter as well as my mother and grandmother.

Now when I was done talking, she said tomorrow her daughter was coming over to see the house because she has not seen it yet, so we started talking about that social service had her taking these class during the daytime because she received TCA, which means "temporary cash assistance" for people who have no income in, so they paid money every month on the third. Depending on if you applied for yourself, you may get $200 to about $300. Now if you apply for you and your child, you may get about $460 to about $500. Now when you start off getting your benefits, they are not going to call you to take the class to help you find a job. They will wait a few months, then send you a letter in the mail letting you know what day you need to report to social service, so you can start your work program. If you don't show up for the class, they will stop your benefits, and you will not receive a check on the third anymore. Now in the class, they ask you what type of job you would like. They help you with your resumé. They help you find the job you are looking for. Say if the job you want to work requires you to take a class and they also charge you for the class. Social services would pay for that. They provide you with all the resources to help you with any job that you want. They pay you for doing this. Now when you start working the job and get your first paycheck, your benefits will stop due to the fact you are now making money. You have a steady income, so you don't need the government assistance no more. By you working, they will close out your account.

Now Tonya was receiving about $500 for her and Damien, and she also was receiving food stamps for her and Damien, about $300 to $400 in food stamps. Now Tonya's rent for her house was $447 a month. Utilities was included in the rent because the house was public housing, which means it goes by your income. Tonya's rent was low because she was in a low-income bracket. After Tonya paid her rent, that would leave her with $53 to her name, plus the food stamps that she was receiving, and the government expect people to be able to survive off a check that does not really leave you with nothing after you pay your bills, but one thing I know is that black people, which is my people, know how to survive. We have been doing it for years. Since our ancestors, we have been surviving with little to nothing, and we have been making it work for us. I watched my grandmother take care of my whole family when I was young with just $60, and everybody in the house was full; nobody was ever hungry. There was not a day I was ever hungry. My grandmother always knew how to survive since a baby, when she came out weighing 3 lb., 9 oz. and was born two months before her actual birthdate.

After me Tonya was done talking about the house and how she wanted me to move in, I said to myself, I don't know about that yet because when you move with a woman, she starts showing you a side of her that you did not see when you were not living with her. I learned that the hard way with my baby mother. I know that moving together is the next step in a relationship to see if you and your partner can make it and then the next step would be marriage, but I say living with your partner, both of you all got to be willing to sacrifice. If not, it's not going to work, and what I mean by that is that everything should be equal. It's not a woman job to cook and clean. As a man, I cook and clean, and, ladies, it not about what a brother could do for you, it about what you all can build together. When you love that person, you will sacrifice for that person, and that person should do the same. That's what genuine love is. You will find yourself trying to better yourself for that person you love. You will stop doing all the things you used to that you know is wrong. You find yourself changing for the better because all you want to do is to make that person that you love happy, so you start to put away all your childish ways and begin to mature. When you find that person that has changed you for the better, that person is a keeper because you will meet that person only once in a lifetime. God gives you this opportunity only once, to have this kind of love, to see what you are going to do with the love, whether you are going to do right by the love or mess over that person that genuinely loves you. When you do realize what you had, it will too late, and you will be looking for that type of love for the rest of your life. You will be wishing and hoping that the next person you meet has a pinch of genuine, unconditional love. When God put you with the person he intended for you to be with for the rest of your life, and you just mess over that love, you will be searching for that type of love and will never find it again because it only comes once in a lifetime. You see people that have been married thirty to forty years, and it was genuine love. When their spouse dies, they never get remarried because they know that the other half is gone. That love they shared with their spouse, they will not ever find on this earth because it is a once-in-a-lifetime kind of love.

Now I truly loved Tonya, but I could tell her love for me was not the same, but I ignored the obvious. Keep reading, and you will find out why I say she did not love me the same as I loved her.

So we were talking about me moving, and she was talking about me helping her get her house. I told her, "I did do that because I wanted to move with you. I did it because I love you, and if your housing had not come through, I still was going to pay the security deposit and the first month's rent so you and your kids could move out your cousin's living room. I love you. As long as I got it, you got it. But I am not ready to move in."

She said, "But that is the next step of our relationship."

I said, "That's true. It doesn't have to be rushed. You just moved in. But I am going to put furniture in the house when I get my money back. If I love you, I will give you my last. I will die for you, I will kill for you." I loved her. I loved everything about her, bad and good, even though she didn't feel the same about me. I could not help that. Call me what you want. When you genuinely love someone, you put up with a lot of bullshit. I put a few good women through ups and downs, so you know what happens. Karma's a bitch. What goes around comes back around. I take full responsibility for my actions as a man. That's a part of showing growth.

Now one month later, I would move in with Tonya, which was the month of May, but I always had that feeling that it would be a bad decision that would change my life. Now I had still paid my grandmother rent for that month just in case all was not good, but it was all good because it was the beginning stages of us living together.

When I moved in, I got DirecTV through the whole house. It was in stages. I went through building the house up to the way we wanted it, so we went a little while with no furniture in the house until I got my taxes money. My state money came back fast. My federal took a little while. I don't know why, but it did, so when I moved in with Tonya, I said I would pay the rent, the cable bill, and our cell phone bill because I was with AT&T, and I added her to my plan, but she said no, we were going to split the rent. I said okay. She paid $225, and I paid $225. I had my grandmother order me a TV from Walmart, and I would pay her cash for it and she did not mind. She had credit with Walmart. I paid her the money the same day she ordered it for me.

Now Tonya was very clean. She would get up and clean. She really could not cook much, but the couple of foods she did know how to cook, she mastered it to a tee. The food was good. I remember waking up in the morning to see Tonya preparing for her day. She would be up ironing her clothes. After, she would hang them on a hanger so they would not get wrinkly, then she would get in the shower and brush her teeth. After she would get out the shower, she would flat iron her hair, then she would put on her makeup. Tonya loved to look good. She would be clean from head to toe, and she loved her a nice pocketbook. She had black heavy-duty bags filled with designer pocketbooks, such as Coach pocketbooks and Michael Kors pocketbooks. She loved a Coach pocketbook. She used to have me laugh because every two to three days, she would change her pocketbook. Tonya loved to look good. When she left the house, she would be looking good from head to toe. She would be smelling so good too.

Bryant would make sure Damien was good. He would wake him up for school and make sure he was good, but he used to try and bully him. He would try and tell him what to do, and when Damien did not do what he said, he would try to put his hands on Damien, but Damien was not going for that, so one particular evening, Tonya had gone out shopping for some things, so it was me, Damien, and Keith. Bryant was in the house too. He was all high up off the oxycodone. He said something slick to Damien, so Damien said, "Yeah, ARD, and you are a bitch."

Now them brothers got to fighting, and that bitch, I am not going to lie, Damien was a little dude, but he had heart like a big dude, so Bryant lift him up and slammed him through the table. This shit was so crazy. While Bryant was lifting Damien up to throw him through the table, Damien was punching Bryant in the face. It's like these brothers were fighting in the air. So when Bryant put Damien through the table, Damien got right up and start punching Bryant in the face. Me and Keith broke the fight up, so Bryant went outside. Now my baby mother dropped my daughter off. When Bryant left the house, Damien went in his room and took his TV and the DirecTV box out his room, so when Bryant came back and went in his room and saw his shit was gone, he went to Damien's room, but he was in me and Tonya's room watching TV. I was downstairs in the kitchen with my daughter when I heard them fighting again, so I ran upstairs to break them up. When I got up there, Bryant was choking Damien with the grip of life; it was like he was trying to kill his little brother, and the whole time, Damien was punching him in the face. This brother was so high the punches were not fazing him. He still was choking him, so I broke both of them up. I was pushing Bryant out the room and pushing Damien back in the room, and the whole time breaking them up, these brothers were still throwing punches, and I was in the middle. As I was pushing them, my daughter was walking to me and Tonya's room where these brothers were still throwing punches.

I said to both of them, "If any of you brothers accidentally hit my daughter, I am going to start throwing punches myself," so they both calmed down. Bryant went in his room and was eating cereal, and Damien remained in me and Tonya's room watching TV, so I said, "Bryant, what, you're high off of oxycodone and weed?"

He said, "Yeah."

I could hear the front door unlocking, then opening. It was Tonya I could hear her walking to the kitchen. I was at the top of the upstairs I could hear her say when she got in the kitchen, "What the fuck happened to the table?" so she came upstairs.

I said, "What up, baby?"

She said, "Do not 'what up, baby' me. What happened to the kitchen table?"

I said, "Baby, I don't have any clue what happened to the kitchen table," so she asked Damien. He said the same thing, so she asked Bryant. He said he didn't know, so we all gave her the same answer that we did not know.

So she said, "I see you motherfuckers are covering up about what happened to the kitchen table. Okay, I am going to find out what happened."

It was about 9:00 p.m., so I had put my daughter to sleep. When Tonya wanted to go for a late-night walk, I said, "We can go. I still do not know what happened to the kitchen table. I am sticking with my story."

She said, "Boy, I am not worried about that no more."

I said to myself, *Yeah. We'll see.* So we left the house and started walking toward East Baltimore. We stopped at the tennis court that's across the street from the light rail, which is next to the culture center. There was a bench over there, so we sat down and started talking. As we get further into the conversation, out of nowhere, she said, "Baby, do you love me?"

I said, "Baby, words cannot explain how much I love you."

She said, "Well, tell me what happened to the kitchen table."

I said, "Baby, I truly love you, but I do not know what happened to the kitchen table."

I would give it to her. She was determined to find out what happened to the kitchen table, so she said, "You don't have to tell me what happened. I know who to call."

I am looking like, *Who the hell she about to call now?*

When she made the phone call, she put the phone on speaker so I could hear the person on the other end, and that person was her oldest son, Keith, so she asked Keith if he was at the house earlier, and he said yes, he was there. She asked him if he knew what happened to the kitchen table, and he told her what happened. This brother said Bryant and Damien were fighting, and Bryant put Damien through the table. I was shaking my head I said to myself. This is their oldest brother, and he's telling this. Should have been a red flag for me.

Keep on reading the story to see why I say that. Tonya said thanks for telling her what happened, and they both said they loved each other and hung up the phone So when she got off the phone, she said, "I told you I was going to find out what happened."

I said to myself, this shit was crazy, so when she was talking about Jamal and Bryant helping around the house, she was talking about them paying her something for them staying there. She said, "I am not taking care of them. They are grown." She had a point there. She was saying the first of the month, she wanted rent from them. Even though we were paying all the bills, she still wanted them to contribute something, so she said she was going to let them know the next day. Me and Tonya started to walk back home.

When we got to the house, everyone was in their rooms. Jamal had come home while me and Tonya were on our walk, so she looked and the room and asked Jamal where he been. He said he had been over Glen's house chilling with Jessie and Ronald. He said they were getting fucked up smoking weed and drinking. He said Glen, Tonya's cousin, said, "Go home. You don't live here anymore." When me and Tonya went in our room, Kiwi was still knocked out asleep, so me and Tonya watched a little TV then we went to sleep.

The next morning, I woke up and made breakfast for everyone—cheese, eggs, bacon, French toast, and fried potatoes—so after everyone was done eating, Tonya called a family meeting, and she was telling them that the first of the month, she wanted $200 from Bryant as well as $200 from Jamal. She said, "Damien, you are to clean up around the house, as well as Bryant and Jamal." She was giving them the rundown on what she expected from them, then she asked if any of them had any questions.

Bryant said, "Yeah, Ma, you being money hungry."

Jamal said, "We are not working nowhere," yet she said, "You all are going to contribute something to the house. You all are grown," so after the family meeting was over, I got Kiwi as well as myself dressed, and we went and saw my mother and my grandmother. When we got over to my grandmother's house, they were excited about seeing their Kiwi doodle.

We chilled over at my grandmother's house for about two hours, then we made our way back over West Baltimore. When we got back to the house, I put cartoons on for Kiwi and began to prepare dinner. Tonya was cleaning up the bathroom upstairs as well as the hallway. I made fried chicken, greens, homemade macaroni and cheese. When I was done, I made everyone's plate, and they came and got their plates. I made Kiwi doodle a plate, and she ate her food. When she was done eating, I cleaned up behind her. After she ate, I ran her a bubble bath. She loved her bubble baths. She would play with the bubbles until they were gone. After she was done taking her bath, I put her to bed, so me and Tonya got in the shower together. After we got out, I dried her off in the bathroom, and I dried myself, and we got dressed. We brushed our teeth and went in the room and went to sleep. When I woke up the next morning, Tonya had made breakfast for everyone. Now after we ate breakfast, me and Tonya watched TV, then I got Kiwi dressed to take her back over her mother's house because I had to work the next day, which was Monday. After I got Kiwi dressed, I went in the bathroom and got dressed, so before I left, I gave Tonya a hug and a kiss and told her I will see her when I get back into the house.

Me and Kiwi, we went and caught the 21 bus to the light rail that was going to BWI. When the light rail arrived, we got on, then we got off at Patapsco station. We caught the 64 to Brooklyn. When we got to her mother's house, I knocked, and she opened the door, and Kiwi went in the house. I told her, "I will come pick her up the Friday coming up."

She said okay. Now me and my baby mother did have problems when we were together, but she is a great mother. I didn't have baby mother drama as people say. All she asked out of me was to take care of our daughter. She didn't have to ask me because I was doing that already. So after I gave Kiwi a hug and told her I loved her, I went to the bus stop and waited on the 64 bus to arrive. When the bus arrived, I got on it, and it took me back to Patapsco station. I got back on the light rail going toward Hunt Valley, which is going back and to the city.

The next stop was Cherry Hill. The train stopped to let the people off the light rail, and before the door could close, this dude just started beating the shit out of the dude who was sitting at the front of the light rail. The dude who was getting his ass whipped got up and took off running to the back of the light rail, so the dude who was whipping the other dude went running behind him and started whipping his ass again. Now the next stop was Westport. The dude whipped the other dude's ass all the way to the next stop. When the doors opened up, the dude took off running again, this time off the light rail. The dude who was whipping the other dude's ass took off running after him. I don't know what that dude did to have him whip his ass like he did, but whatever it was, the dude whipped and chased him off the light rail. On the train, the light rail, or the bus, you never know who you are going to run into. Baltimore city is a small city. You are bound to run into whoever you are beefing with, and that's what looks like what happened on the light rail that day.

When I arrived home and went in the house, I could smell loud, which is weed, so I went in the kitchen and made me a sandwich, then I went upstairs. When I got to the top of the stairs, I looked in Jamal's room. It was a hell lot of smoke, so much smoke that it was coming out into the hallway. Just by walking through the hallway, you could catch a contact high. It was only Tonya and Jamal in there smoking, so I went in me and Tonya's room, and I got my clothes ready for work the next day. When I was finished getting my clothes ready, I started to watch TV.

Tonya and Damien got into an argument about school, so she told Damien to go to his room. When he went to his room, he slammed the door and locked it. She said, "You don't pay no bills in here, so you don't have the right to shut slam or lock any doors in this house." She told him to clean up his damn room too.

When Tonya came in the room, I could tell she was pissed off because she was red-hot, and what I mean by that was Tonya was a redbone, so when she came in the room, she was ten times redder then her actual skin color. You ever seen one of them cartoons where the character gets so mad they turn red until steam begins to come from the top of the cartoon character's head? That's how Tonya would be when she would get mad, when someone would pissed her off. She was so red I said I was going to touch her forehead to see how hot she was, and when I touched her head, I got burned like if I touched the stove when the flames are on. So I told her, "Baby, calm down now." Tonya had high blood pressure, so her being that angry was not good for her health.

Damien got his mother back by bursting in the room and telling her, "You don't have the right to close no doors," so Tonya was like, "Close the door." He walked off saying, "You don't have the right to have any doors closed," and did not shut the door, so I got up and closed the door. That shit was crazy. I am still, to this day, trying to find out how in the hell everyone else in the house had locks on their door and me and Tonya room did not.

Tonya and I started kissing again when this brother Damien opened the door again. Tonya jumped up and went to grab a belt out the closet. Damien got out of there and ran to his room and locked the door. He was laughing hard, so Tonya was like, "Damien, open the door," so Damien was like, "Why would I do that?"

Tonya said, "That's okay. I am going to get you. You cannot stay in there forever," so Damien said, "Ma, I apologize. I was playing through the door," so Tonya was like, "I don't want to hear it. I am going to get you," so I said to Tonya when she came back into the room, "Do you want me to pick the lock on the door so you can get that little brother?"

She said, "Yeah, go ahead," so what I did was I went and got a butter knife from downstairs in the kitchen. When I came back upstairs, Damien had the music up loud. He was playing Call of Duty on his PlayStation 3. I picked the lock, and before I could say, "Baby, the door is unlocked," she had already burst in the room. If you could only see the look on Damien's face when Tonya burst in the room. The look on his face said it all. That brother looked like, How the fuck she got in the room? When she burst in the room, that brother Damien jumped out his skin. I was laughing like a motherfucker. That shit was funny. That dude was so caught off guard to the point Tonya said she was not going to whip his ass with the belt, so me and Tonya just went back into the room and watched TV.

Bryant had an older woman who Tonya really didn't like because she felt that she was too old for her son, so I said, "How you are going to say that when you are twenty years older than me? How you think my mother would feel about that?"

She said, "You got a point there," but she said she still didn't like her, and later she would find out she had good reason not to like her. Continue to read the story to see why I said that. Bryant and his older lady came into the house and went in his room, so I ordered pizza for everyone from Pizza Boli's. Everyone ate. I went upstairs and went to bed. I woke up the next morning, washed my face, brushed my teeth, and got dressed. I went and caught the 21 bus to the 35 bus stop.

When I got to work, I unloaded a truck of 110-pound bags of black pepper and a twenty-footer of canned apples. When I was done unloading both trucks, I went in the bathroom and washed under my arms and my chest so I would not stink so bad when I went and got on the bus. The black pepper smell was hard to get out of the clothes, so I changed out of the clothes that I would work in, and even after I changed my clothes and put the work clothes in my book bag you could still smell that black pepper; the smell was so strong that when I would get on the bus and walk past or sit next to someone, they still could smell that black pepper. That's how strong it was.

I got on the 35 bus. This bus stand crowded in the morning. Everyone who had to go to work caught that bus. That bus stayed crowded to the point people would be packed from the back all away to the front of the bus. Everyone who got on the bus earlier before the bus got crowded, they got all the seats, and the people who got on after all the seats were taken them, people would have to stand until a seat became available.

Now after I got off the 35 bus, I walked to the 21 bus stop. That bus didn't get as crowded as the 35 bus, so I waited on the bus, then I said, "I am going to go to my grandmother house," so I walked around the corner and made sure my grandmother and my mother was okay. I stayed around there for about an hour, then I went and caught the 21 bus.

When I got home, I went and made myself something to eat, and then I went and got into the shower. I ate my food. Now Tonya was not home yet.

That Saturday was Mother's Day. I had an idea of what Tonya wanted for Mother's Day. She wanted a pocketbook and money, so I ordered her a Coach pocketbook, and I hid the pocketbook in the house. She had no idea I got paid that Friday. I would put $300 in her new pocketbook as well. I was cooking her dinner that Sunday. I was going to make her crab cakes, fried cabbage, and potato salad. That Friday after I got off work, I was going to the market to pick up the food so I can be prepared for Sunday. My plans for that week was all set.

After I was done eating, I took my plate downstairs and washed the dishes. I heard the front door being unlocked. It was Damien coming in the house from school. I said, "What's up?"

He said, "What's up?" and asked if his mother was home. I said, "No, she's not home yet," so I went upstairs and watched TV. About a half hour later, Tonya came home. She came upstairs, and she said, "Hello, baby, how was your day at work?"

I said, "Good." I asked her how her day was. She said to keep receiving her TCA, she had to volunteer at a day care center. Instead of her going to social services and sitting in a class all day, all she had to do now to keep her benefits was report to the day care center every Monday through Friday and every Friday before she leaves the daycare center, to get the woman who was running the center to sign her papers stating that she has been there Monday through Friday so she could take them back to social services so they would not cut her benefits off. I said to myself, *There's got to be a better way to make a living because that is too much.* "You are going through a lot to keep only $500 in money and $300 in food stamps. That shit is crazy."

After we got done talking, Tonya went and got in the shower. I called my mother and talked to her for a while. She was telling me how she was moving out my grandmother's house and moving over to Cornell's daughter's house. She said she was tired of my grandmother and her rules, that nothing was ever good enough for her. She could clean the house from top to bottom. She goes and play her numbers and get her scratch-offs a hundred times a day my mother also helped paid bills in the house as well she said she felt like nothing was never good enough, so she was just going to move she said she already moved some of her stuff out of the house over Sharon's house. Now Sharon had a lot of mental health issues for real when she did not take her medication, my mother said when they went over the house, it really needed to be cleaned up. She said it smells bad in the house. She said the reason she moved over there was to help her with the kids. She felt bad for the kids because Sharon would get mad and beat the kids beyond a butt whipping—she was trying to push them down the stairs, yanking their arms like she was trying to break their arms. Sharon was fucked up in the head, so my mother moved in the house to take some of the stress off her. Larry was the kids' father. He had mental health issues as well, but his mental health issues were not as bad as Sharon's because before my mother moved in the house, Larry would make sure the kids were good. Now my mother was there in Cornell, they had more help around the house, so my mother knew Cornell ever since Lafayette project. They used to go together, but Cornell had gotten locked up for two attempted murders. He served a total of twenty-five to thirty years in prison. Cornell was locked up so long, his son got locked up, and he ran into them in jail. He was locked up with two of his sons. By him not being able to be in his son's life, they ended up going down the path that he went down. Their life could have been different, but you never know the outcome until it happened. I believe we are put on this earth for a reason, but we don't know what the reason is until God wants us to know or until God reveals our purpose. What is the reason for our existence? Everyone is born with a story, with a purpose. We live our story out until the day we die. Your story may be to help people before you die. The next person purpose may be to destroy as many people as they can before they die. Before you leave this earth, you will find out what your purpose is.

So my mother ran back into Cornell, and they started talking again and decided they wanted to get back together. She had another call coming in on the phone, so she said she would call me back So I told her I love her. Now my cousin and his baby mother and their two kids moved out my grandmother house as well my brother Nathan moved out my brother Nathan is bisexual. He was going with a transgender man, and they moved in together. My grandmother was my brother's payee my brother was receiving a check from social security for his disability, so my grandmother was the payee because one of my brother disability he could not manage his money, so my grandmother was supposed to help him manage his money, so my grandmother mother was only giving my brother $200 a month and telling him to get everything he needed for that month with that $200 So my brother asked my grandmother for more money he said $200 is not enough money to get through a hole month, so my grandmother said no she said he was lucky that she gave him $200 now my grandmother was receiving $720 a month for my brother and she was his payee and she told my brother after she pay him his $200. That leaves her with $520. She told my brother the rest of that money was rent for him staying there, using the BGE and water as well as food, so my brother was like, That is not right, which it was not right. My brother was twenty-three years old at that time, but he was being treated like a kid, so he told my grandmother that he was just going to change her as his payee, so my grandmother said if he went up there to change her as his payee, he could get out her house. My brother said that was cool with him. He said he was planning to move anyway.

So my brother told his transgender partner what happened. He said that he would be his payee. Now the transgender that my brother was talking to had to find a place to move, so my brother and him, they were planning to get a place together. They made appointments to social security and went up and ended up freezing the check, which means they put the check on hold, and they changed the payee as well. They made an appointment with my brother and my grandmother as well as my brother's partner that was going to be the new payee. Whatever my brother told them people up in social security, they were upset with my grandmother.

That next month's check came out on a Saturday. Anytime a check came out on a weekend such as Saturday or Sunday, people who got their checks on the first of the month would get their check that Friday instead. They didn't freeze the check in time, so my grandmother ended up getting the check, so my brother asked her if she could give him his money, so my grandmother said, "I am not giving you a thing," so my brother was like, "I got you. I am going to call social security."

My grandmother said, "Bitch, you can get the hell out my house."

My brother said, "You cannot just put me out. You got to give me thirty to ninety days. You got to go downtown and file an eviction notice."

When my brother said that, that pissed my grandmother off even more, so my brother went to his appointment up social security that Monday, and he told them that my grandmother received the check for that month and that my grandmother stole his money. They were threatening to have my grandmother arrested. They told her if she did not give him his money, they were going to send the police to the house. My brother had social security to call my grandmother's phone while he was still there. When the social security representative was talking to my grandmother, my brother was in the background saying, "I don't want my grandmother to be arrested. I just want my money."

When my brother got to my grandmother's house, he knocked on the door. My grandmother opened the door. She told him he had thirty days to find another place. He said okay. She gave him some of the money back and told him the money that she was keeping was for him staying there that month. My brother ended up moving with his transgender boyfriend, so it was just my grandmother and my little brother living in a three-story house by themselves.

After Tonya got out the shower, so she got to talking about Chantelle and her baby's father. "He doesn't help her with their daughter." She said her daughter was taking care of Kevin, Chantelle's baby's father's name as well as their daughter. She was taking care of both of them. She said Kevin was a weed head. All he wanted to do was smoke weed all day. She said Kevin's mother's sister had money and got money put up for Kevin and his daughter. She said Kevin's mother and his aunt spoiled his daughter and that Kevin didn't want to get a job. He just wanted to live off her daughter and his aunt.

I said, "That shit crazy."

I could tell Tonya really didn't fuck with Kevin, and she felt her daughter could do better. She said, "Chantelle when she goes to work, she got to pay him to watch his own daughter. He doesn't even watch his own daughter—his mother or his aunt watch his daughter."

I said, "That's fucked up. A man takes care of his responsibility as a man."

So Tonya was so upset she was turning red again.

I said, "Baby, calm down." She wanted Chantelle to leave him income, move home. Where Kevin's aunt lived at was over there near Morgan, the college, which is a neighborhood where people with money live at. People who owned their homes live at a middle-class neighborhood, and we were living in the project public housing. Chantelle was not moving back to that lifestyle. Tonya really didn't like Kevin because while Chantelle was pregnant with their daughter, Kevin went out and cheated on Chantelle and got another woman pregnant, so since then Tonya cannot stand Kevin.

Chantelle has a beautiful heart. If she loves or if she just fucks with you, she's not going to let no one talk bad about you. She will fight for you. Her love is genuine, but if you take her kindness for weakness, she will go from 0 to 100 real quick, no lie.

So after Tonya calmed down, we watched TV. Tonya liked watching reality TV shows with a bunch of drama, such as the *Housewives of Atlanta* or *Love & Hip Hop*. Now I like watching ID (Investigation Discovery) channel, which has a bunch of killing shows that are based on a true story. Tonya did not like watching anything on that channel, and I did not like watching the *Housewives of Atlanta* or *Basketball Wives*. She used to watch the stories too, such as *the Young and the Restless, the Bold and the Beautiful.* I used to laugh. Every time something would happen on one of them television shows, Tonya would get on the phone and call one of her homegirls, and they would talk about what happened on the TV show, so after I was done watching television, I went to sleep. Tonya continued to watch television, then she got up and went downstairs.

I had to get up and go to work the next day. I got up, washed my face, brushed my teeth, put on my clothes, and caught the 21 to the 22. I was going to Overflow warehouse over there on Grays Road. There were two furniture trucks that needed to be unloaded, so I unloaded one truck, and Troy unloaded the other. When we were done unloading, me and Troy went and caught the 22 to the 21.

When I got home, I washed me and Tonya's clothes and straightened up our room, and I took a shower. I got dressed and got the clothes out of the washing machine and hung the clothes up around the house because we did not have a dryer at the time and it was summer, so the clothes would dry fast. We didn't need any dryer. The house was so hot it would dry the clothes quicker than the dryer machine would. After I was done hanging the clothes, I went upstairs and watched TV. We did not have everything, but God blessed us with enough, and we were surviving. As I was watching TV, I heard the front door being unlocked, and I yelled downstairs, "Who is that?" It was Damien. He ran upstairs and was like, "Q, you wanna try to play Madden?"

I said, "Yeah, we can play Madden, so I picked New England Patriots. That is my favorite NFL team. He picked the Baltimore Ravens. We played two games of Madden. I won one game; he won one game. So after we played Madden, I introduced him to NBA 2K12. At that time, I was nicer and NBA 2k than Madden, and Damien did not even know about NBA 2K12. He said all he was play-ing was Call of Duty and Madden. Now Damien had a PlayStation 3, and I had an Xbox 360. I have always been a fan of the Xbox. I worked all summer that I was out of school, and I saved my money up, and I brought the Xbox, but I had every system when I brought the first Xbox, even the green and the black system. I also had the PlayStation 2 and the Nintendo GameCube, and even though I had every system during that time, the Xbox had always been my favorite system since day 1. Damien said he had a PlayStation 2, so we played a game of NBA 2K12. I picked the Lakers because that's my favorite NBA team. Kobe Bryant is the greatest basketball player. He is my favorite basketball player. If you ask me, out of these three NBA all-stars, who I would pick to play on my NBA team, it would be

(1) Michael Jordan, (2) Kobe Bryant, and (3) Lebron James. I am picking Kobe Bryant every time. I feel like Kobe Bryant is better than Jordan and LeBron. So I picked the Lakers, and he picked the Bulls. I destroyed the Bulls with the Lakers. Ever since that day, Damien would always want to play NBA 2K. He started to get even nicer as he began to play the game more. He became so nice he became one of the highest-ranked NBA 2K players in the world. Continue to read to see how he became one of the highest NBA 2K players.

So after I beat him in the game of NBA 2K, I could hear the door being unlocked. I could hear that it was Tonya because she was talking on the phone. She called me downstairs and asked me how my day was. I said good. I asked her how her day was. She said good, considering she had gotten into it with one of the ladies that worked at the day care center, but other than that, her day was good. I saw that she had like five brown boxes. I looked in the boxes, and it was sandwiches and chips. I opened the refrigerator and I saw apple juice and chocolate milk.

I said, "Baby, where did you get these school lunches from?"

She said, "The woman who runs the day care center said any one of the workers at the center could bring home boxes of lunch from the day care center."

She said the woman told her, "After the kids in the day care center eat their food, there's always a lot of food boxes left over as well as milk and juices." She said if nobody takes any of the food home it would all go in the trash can, so Tonya said she would take some boxes home every day so none of the food go to waste.

I said, "Baby, you are crazy. It's also crazy that they would throw the food in the trash when on every corner is a homeless person and many homeless people in the city."

She said her and the two other women at the day care center took lunch boxes home.

I said, "You all crazy." I heard Damien coming downstairs, so Tonya was like, "Damien, how was your day in school?" Damien said it was good then he went in the refrigerator and looked into the brown boxes. He said, "Where'd these boxed lunches come from?"

That's when Tonya told him the same thing she told me So after Tonya and Damien were done talking about them school lunches, Damien grabbed a boxed lunch and a juice and then he went upstairs, so me and Tonya continued to talk downstairs when we heard someone turning the doorknob as they were unlocking the door. It was Bryant, and he walked in the kitchen and said, "What up" to me and Tonya. We said, "what up?" then Tonya asked him where he has been at. He said, "Over East."

Now Bryant used to be over East by Hoffman up there in the area where the carry-out store called Jimmy's was. Jimmy's was a store that had one way in, one way out Now Bryant had a godmother who he had respect for more than his own mother. He would talk to his godmother about a lot of shit more than he would talk to the woman who gave birth to him. That shit was crazy. His godmother had three sons and a daughter, and they looked at Bryant like they were real brothers, or so it seemed. Continue to read to see why I said "or so it seems," because the people you love doesn't always love you back or don't have the same love that you have for them, and these type of people, as soon as you turn your back, will stab you right in the back. Sometimes it's your own family. Sometimes it's the people you look at as if they were your family, and sometimes people that's not your family treat you better than your own flesh and blood, so shit like that makes it hard to truly trust anyone.

Bryant was telling his mother he had beat up some dude over East Baltimore. Now a lot of people were saying Bryant was BGF, which is one of the biggest gangs in Baltimore City. A lot of people were saying he was Muslim in BGF, so Tonya's phone began to ring. She went in the next room and answered the phone, so I continued to talk to Bryant. I told him if he needed any tones, which means guns, my people got the plug on the joints, which means gun. He asked how much. I said $600, brand new, out the box, never even been fired. Before he said okay, I said, "Just let me know. I will give the word to my people to holler."

He said okay, so after me and Bryant was done talking, I went back upstairs to relax and watch TV. After Tonya was done downstairs, she came upstairs and lay on my chest. I went to sleep. When

I woke up the next morning, I heard Tonya waking Damien up for school, so I got up and gave my baby a hug and a kiss, morning breath and all. When you love that person, you do not give a damn about showing your love where or when. You don't give a damn about what people got to say about you and the person that you love, so I kissed Tonya and went in the bathroom, washed my face, brushed my teeth, and got ready to go to work. That day I was going to OST to unload a black pepper truck by myself, so I gave Tonya a hug and a kiss and told her I loved her and I would see her later, so she said, "I love you too. Have a good day at work," and I said, "You too."

I left the house and went got on the 21 bus to the 35 bus. When I had arrived to the warehouse, I had gotten there too early to the point the warehouse was not even opened yet, so I sat down on the chair outside and waited, then the woman that we called Mama arrived to open up the warehouse doors. The warehouse was still dark to the point you could not see what was on the floor. It was a rainy day, so Mama opened the door and went in the warehouse. Next I heard Mama hitting the floor and saying, "Goddamn! Shit, that hurt," so I ran into the warehouse to see what was going on, and I could see Mama had tripped off the plate that one of the forklift operators had left right in the middle of the floor. A plate is what the forklift operators use to be able to get on the truck to move pallets on and off the trucks and also other freight that may not be on pallets, so I helped Mama up off the ground and walked her to her office, and she sat in the chair. It was like God was with her when she fell over the plate because from the sound of it, she hit the ground pretty hard and not one bone was broken, given her age. It was like God cushioned the fall for her. All she had was a little bruise on her arm and her leg, but other than that, she was good to go. The other employees began to arrive, and she asked them, "Which one of you had the bright idea to leave the plate in the middle of the floor?"

Everybody had the dumb look on their face. One of them said, "Why, what happened?" and she said, "What happened? Come look at my arm and my leg. That's what happened. I tripped over the plate. That's what happened."

Everybody said sorry and asked if she was okay. She told them thanks to me getting there extra early, she was okay, so after everybody was done apologizing to Mama, Mike brought me pallets over to the truck so I could start unloading the truck. After I was done unloading the truck, it was about 11:30 am. I went in the bathroom and washed up and put on another change of clothes and then I went and caught the 35 bus to the 21. When I got home, I went upstairs and got in the shower and really got that black pepper smell out of my skin. I washed my dreads three times to really get the smell out of my hair. I got dressed, and I gathered the clothes that needed to be washed and Tonya's clothes as well as Damien's clothes. When I walked past Damien's room, I noticed that his PlayStation 3 was no longer in his room, so I said to myself, *What, he put the game up somewhere?* I went downstairs and began to wash clothes. As I was washing, I could hear the front door being unlocked. It was Damien, so I asked him where his PlayStation 3 was. He said, It's not upstairs?"

I said, "No, it's not upstairs."

Brother ran upstairs so fast you would have thought he was running for team USA, trying to bring home the gold medal. That's how fast he was running. I heard Damien upstairs saying to himself, "Where the fuck is my game at?" You could hear him leaving his room and going into Bryant's room looking for his game, but the game was not in there. Whoever had the game, they took the system and all the games Damien had, which had to be fifty to a hundred games. After Damien got done looking for the system and the games, he came back downstairs. He was beyond mad. That brother looked like he wanted to kill somebody. I said to Damien, "Who you think got the game?"

He said, "I know who got the game. Bryant."

Someone was unlocking the door. Damien thought it was Bryant, but it was Tonya. I asked her how her day was. She said it was good. I gave her a hug and a kiss. She had a big bag that had them school lunches inside. I asked her, "How long do you plan on bringing these lunches home? God has blessed us." She said as long as they kept letting them bring their food home. She said if they didn't take everything home, then it would go into the trash. When she brought the lunch boxes home, somebody was going to eat them as oppose to not bringing them home and the lady that ran the day care center would throw everything in the trash can. I said, "You got a point there."

So Damien asked his mother if she'd seen his PlayStation 3. She said, "No, not since earlier. Why, what happened?"

He told her the game had been upstairs earlier. Now it was gone. Even she herself said, "Bryant got the game."

So Damien anxiously waited until Bryant came walking into the house. Around 10:00 to 11:00 p.m., that's when Bryant walked into the house. Damien asked, "You know where my system and my games are?"

He said, yeah, he took them over his people's house. He said he would bring the game back on Monday, so Damien was like, "Why you had to take all the games if you are just letting them hold the game?"

He said he's going to get the game on Monday. Damien said, "You should have asked if you could hold my game," but turns out that Bryant not only went in Damien's room and took his PlayStation 3, he also went in Jamal's room and stole a phone that Jamal had. Later, Jamal asked him had he seen his phone.

Bryant said, "I don't know where your phone is."

Jamal said, "I know you got my phone."

He said, "Yeah, whatever, and if I do have your phone, what you are going to do?"

Jamal said, "I got you," so after they had their words, everybody went in their room. You would think that it would be the last of it, but it wasn't. The next day was Friday, so after I got off work, I had to go to the market to get the food to prepare for Sunday. Then I went to sleep. When I woke up the next day, I washed my face and brushed my teeth and caught the 21 to the 36. I was going to the Overflow Warehouse on Washington Boulevard to unload a truck of bags of Domino sugar, plus a truck full of glass jars that contained sauerkraut. One thing about this truck, you had to be careful how you lay and stacked them on the pallets. After I was done with both trucks, it was about 2:00 to 2:30 p.m., and I went and washed my chest and under my arms and put deodorant on and another shirt. When I was done, I went outside. Pat, who I worked for at that time, was outside in his all-white Range Rover. It was Friday. Every Friday was payday, so Pat would ride around to all the warehouses that he had a contract for in the city as well as all the warehouse that he had a contract for in the county and drop off everybody's money. One thing I can say about Pat, he never played with nobody's money. Whatever you earned working for him, he would make sure he got your money, even if he makes a mistake with the payroll because he had like 1000 to 1,500 employees. He had a lot of Mexicans working for him. Pat could speak five different languages, so if he made a mistake, he would look at his books and see the error he made and let you know he sees the mistake he made, and the next time he sees you, he will have your money. Every Friday, Pat would have tens of thousands on him. Pat would put everyone's money in an envelope with a receipt of the money you made that week as well as a paper with a list of all the trucks you worked on for that week. Pat ran his business organized. He kept records of the truck numbers,

One day, me, Pat, Troy's cousin, and a couple of Mexicans, we all were working over the warehouse over on Washington Boulevard, and that day was payday which was Friday. There were at least eight to nine trucks over there, so it was a lot of work. Troy's cousin unloaded one truck by himself, and he said he was going to unload another truck with Troy, so when Troy unloaded his truck, he was looking for where his cousin was. Pat had already paid everybody that was working at that warehouse for that week. So Troy was looking for his cousin, but he could not find him anywhere in the warehouse, so he went outside to see if he was smoking a cigarette. When he got outside, he didn't see his cousin, but he noticed that one of windows to Pat's Range Rover was busted out, and the alarm to the car was going off. Troy came back into the warehouse and told Pat that his car window was busted out and that his cousin was nowhere to be found. Pat went out to his car and saw that not only was his window busted out but the white envelope that had money was gone, so he came back in to the warehouse and told Troy to call his cousin's phone.

Troy called, and it went straight to voicemail; he'd turned his phone off. Pat told him that he stole about $5,000 from his car. That was the money he had after he paid everybody. You could tell Pat was pissed off. He told Troy one or two things would happen: his cousin could bring the money back and the money that he owed his cousin for next week would go to replace the window to his car, or he doesn't bring the money back and Pat would press charges and get him arrested and he could use that money that he stole to pay for lawyer fees and bail money.

Troy said, "Pat, you know my family members are all fucked-up individuals. You might as well go ahead and press charges because my cousin is not going to bring the money back," so Pat said, "I am going to give him the chance to make it right. When you go home today, deliver my message."

Troy said, "I will." You could tell that Troy was pissed off. I knew myself that Troy's cousin was not going to bring that money back. That was a major sum of money. That money was going in to the street whether it was weed or he was going to buy some weight.

So I ended up throwing the other truck with Troy. He said that was exactly why he didn't vouch for his family such as his cousin. He said the only person on his father's side of the family was his grandmother, that she was the only one. He said the rest of his family could just drop dead for all he cared. That's how wrong they had done him. Troy lived with his grandmother and his cousins and uncle, and everybody got high in the house. Some of them smoked crack. Some of them shot dope. Some of them did both. They would steal a lot of Troy's stuff as well as the grandmother's stuff. Troy's grandmother was old school. She believed in saving every dime that she worked hard for, so she had money. She owned that house that they were living in on Biddle Street, and she owned a house up on Preston Street as well. She had land down South and properties that she owned down South as well. One day, one of Troy's cousin, his grandmother's grandson, decided that he didn't have any way to make his money but to rob his seventy-year-old grandmother by gunpoint. That shit was fucked up. That could not have been my grandmother. That dude would be no longer living, so Troy grandmother's ended up pressing charges only to defend him after she found out they were trying to give him twenty to thirty years, so she went to court and spoke on his behalf, saying she didn't want him to do any jail time, that he needed help with his drug problem, that they should give him rehab. Troy said he was pissed off with his grandmother because she should have let him get the time. He said that would have been one less problematic family member. His cousin ended up getting some time, but it was not for the charges of robbing his grandmother. He got about two to three years. Troy's family members gave him and his grandmother problems. They always had their hand out begging for money, not wanting to earn their own money and instead depending on him and his grandmother for everything.

So after Troy told his cousin what Pat said, he did like I said he would, which was *not* give the money to Troy so Troy could give the money back to Pat. He kept the money, but I think Troy paid Pat the money back or the grandmother because Pat did not press charges and Troy's cousin ended up working back out there like nothing happened about nine months after he stole the money from Pat's car.

So I went outside, and Pat was in the car counting money, so he called me to come get my money. Now every time we would get paid, we would have to sign a receipt. We would get a copy, and Pat would get a copy, and this would let him know who got paid as well. I made $600 that week, but taxes were taken out, so I made about $540. After I signed the receipt and got my money, I went and caught the 36 to the 21. I went to the house and dropped my book bag and went down to the Save A Lot that was right in the front of our house on Dolphin Street. I got everything I needed to prepare Tonya a Mother's Day meal. After I was done, I went back into the house and put everything in the refrigerator, and I went upstairs and got in the shower. When I got out, I got dressed, then I went downstairs and washed clothes. I could hear someone unlock the front door. It was Damien.

I said, "What up, Damien? How was your day at school?"

He said it was good. He asked was I trying to play the game the Xbox 360? He wanted to play NBA 2K as well as Madden, so I said, "Yeah, you can lose real fast." I told him go set up the game. I said I wanted to play with the Lakers, so I started the washing machine and went upstairs. I had the Lakers. Damien was playing with the Bulls, so of course you know the Lakers beat the Bulls. After the Lakers beat the Bulls, he picks the Miami Heat and I picked the Lakers again. Each game that we would play, Damien would get even nicer. He would still lose but not as badly, so after the Lakers got another victory, we played two games of Madden. I won one game; he won a game.

I could hear someone coming through the front door. It was Tonya. She had a big bag of them damn school box lunches. She came upstairs. We were still playing Madden, so I asked her how her day was. She said good. She asked me the same. I said good, so she asked Damien how his day was at school. He said it was cool. She asked him what he learned today. He said, "A lot."

She said, "What do you mean a lot?"

He said the same thing, which was "I learned a lot."

She said, "Do you have any homework?"

He said, "No, I did my homework in school."

Me and Tonya both said, "Bullshit" at the same time. He was not telling the truth, so Tonya was like, "Let me see the homework you did in school."

He said, "I left my book bag in school with my homework," so Tonya said, "When you come home from school on Monday, you better have your book bag and some work that you did for that day as well as some homework for that day."

Damien said okay. After we were done playing Madden, I told Damien he could take the Xbox in his room and play Call of Duty. He said okay. After Damien left the room, me and Tonya got to talking about Bryant. She was saying, "He doesn't listen. You cannot tell him anything because he thinks he knows it all."

I said, "Baby, he is gone to the street. All you can do now is get a life insurance policy for him and pray for him and leave it in God's hands."

I knew that sounded harsh, but Bryant had no regard for anyone. He was the true definition of *coldhearted*. He was a young brother and was heartless. He was very intelligent. It was like he just lost all hope in life. You know how people say people who lose all hope in life don't care whether they live or die? That was Bryant's mindset. He didn't give a fuck about anything. That's why all she could do was pray for him and give it to God.

After me and Tonya were done talking, I went downstairs and cooked hamburgers and fries for me, Tonya, and Damien. I used ground beef to make my burgers. I made homemade French fries. I cut the skin off the potatoes, and I sliced them into the shape of fries and then fried them. It was only me Tonya and Damien in the house. Jamal was gone as well as Bryant, so after I was done cooking, I made Tonya and Damien a plate and took them their food.

Now Damien did not have a gift to give his mother on Mother's Day, so I told him that the gift I was giving his mother tomorrow came from both of us. I told him to sign the card, and we were going to present it to her tomorrow, so he signed the card. I signed the card. I put the money into the card and sealed it up, so after I was done with that, I put the gift up so she would not find it, then I went back upstairs and lay next to Tonya. We watched TV and talked, then Chantelle called and told her she would be over tomorrow to chill with her on Mother's Day. Tonya was very excited about spending time with her daughter.

I could hear the door being unlocked. Someone was coming in the house, then we heard somebody say, "Mama?" and they started coming up the stairs. It was Keith and Shamika. Now Shamika, from what Tonya told me about her, was a damn good woman, and from what I could see, she was beautiful. Keith would treat her like she was not. Shit, he would cheat on her, verbally abuse her, make her feel like she was nothing. Keith wanted to wish his mother an early happy Mother's Day. He brought her a gift that was from him and Shamika. Now Tonya really loved Shamika like she was her daughter, and she would get on Keith about how he was treating her. It was not right. Keith thought he was the man. He was a clown. I don't even know how the Piru allowed this brother to even become Piru. Continue to read the story to see why I said that.

Now Tonya gave Shamika a hug as well as Keith. I said "what up" to both of them. Keith asked her where Jamal and Bryant was at. She said, "Jamal is over Glen's house with Jessie," and she did not know where Bryant was. Keith was talking to Damien. He asked him where his PlayStation 3 was. Damien was like, "That Bryant let one of his homeboys hold the game into Monday. That man did not even ask me if it was cool if he could allow his homeboy to hold the game. When I came home from school, my shit was gone."

His mother heard him and yelled, "Boy, you better watch your mouth. You are not grown!"

Keith was like, "That's crazy. Bryant not right for that."

Keith and Bryant did not really get along, and they really were not on good terms. After Keith was done talking to Damien, him and Shamika left. Keith lived in the high-rise apartment on McCollum, which is right up the street from Tonya's house. It was public housing. His apartment went by his income. He was receiving a check from social security for his disability as well. He thought he was a trapper/rapper, which means he would sell drugs, but also he would go to the studio and record music that would be pure trash. He recorded a mixtape. One song on the whole mixtape was cool, and that was the one where he had his sister, Chantelle, sing the hook on the song. That song was the best song on the mixtape. The rest of it was trash. Before, they started to call rappers mumble rapper. Keith was a mumble rapper. The brother be yelling on every song. The mixtape was just trash, in my opinion, but you could not tell Tonya that. She was playing that mixtape every day. She was proud of her son's mixtape.

After Keith and Shamika left, me and Tonya went upstairs and watched TV. I went to sleep, and I woke up the next morning and went and made breakfast for everyone and took Tonya her food as well as the stuff me and Damien brought her. I woke her up. I said, "Happy Mother's Day! Here's your breakfast," so after she ate her breakfast, she opened up the boxes, and she pulled out the paper that was in the boxes. She saw the Coach pocketbook and went crazy. If you could see the look on her face, she was so happy. She took the pocketbook out the box and took the plastic that was wrapped around it. You know how people are when they get a new pair of shoes, how they smell their shoes and be like, "There is no smell like that new shoe smell"? Well, Tonya did that with her new pocketbook.

She said, "There is no smell like that new pocketbook smell."

I burst out laughing, so I said, "Baby, go ahead and open your new pocketbook," so she opened it. She saw it was two cards and opened the first card. She saw the money and was very happy, then she read the card and said, "Aww, baby, thanks for everything," then she opened the other card and saw the money. If you could see the look on her face, it said it all.

I said, "Happy Mother's Day, baby. You deserve it all, baby. We appreciate you, baby. Now you got money to go in your new Coach pocket."

Damien came in the room and said, "Happy Mother's Day."

Tonya said, "Thank you, Damien," then her phone begin to ring. It was Chantelle. She wished Tonya a happy Mother's Day. She said she would be over the house sometime that day. So after Tonya got off the phone with Chantelle, she called her mother and wished her a happy Mother's Day, and she told her about the gift that me and Damien got her.

Her mother was like, "You got a new pocketbook and money to go in your new pocket? When do I get to meet this young man who's bringing my daughter so much happiness?"

She said, "Soon, very soon."

Now Mother Tones and Father Tones are Christians for real. They stay in the church; they stay in the Good Book. If you look up the definition of *Christian* in the dictionary, you would see a picture of Mother Tones and Father Tones. They are in church every Sunday. Every time their church had any service, they are there. I told Tonya to tell her mother happy Mother's Day and that I had two cards for her. Tonya's mother said thank you, and she asked Tonya if she was coming to church the next day. Tonya said she would be there.

After Tonya got off the phone with her mother, she called all her homegirls and wished them a happy Mother's Day. After she got done bragging to all her homegirls about her Coach pocketbook and her money, Jamal called her and wished her a happy Mother's Day.

After Tonya was done talking to everybody, she went and got in the shower.

So Damien was like, "Q, you trying to play NBA 2K?"

I said, "You can lose real fast," so he said, "I am not going to lose this time."

I said, "We are about to find out." You know who I picked—the Lakers. He picked the Bulls. It was a close game. I won by three points, so we played another game. That game also was close, but I still won. Damien said, "The game we play be close compared to when I first started playing NBA 2K."

I said, "Yeah, because you are getting a little nicer."

He said, "You know what, that means it's only a matter of time before I beat you in a game."

I said, "Keep hope alive," so after we were done playing NBA 2K, we played Call of Duty: Modern Warfare survival mode. After, Tonya asked me to go to the store. She wanted two Pepsis, some sunflower seeds, as well as some chips, so I went to the market across from the house. Me and Damien walked to the market, and I told him to get what he wanted from the store. After we got everything from the store, we went up front to the cashier. I paid for everything, and we left. When we got back into the house, Tonya was downstairs listening to Keith's mixtape, listening to the song that Keith had made with his sister. She loved that song. Me and Damien took the bags into the kitchen. We could hear somebody unlocking the door. It was Chantelle and Mama and Kevin. She came into the house yelling, "Mama, where you at?"

Tonya was like, "Girl, why you are yelling? I am right here in the kitchen." Tonya was putting the things away that we got from the market, so Chantelle brought her mother some cards and balloons, and she said she loved her and happy Mother's Day. That dude Kevin said, "What up?"

I said, "What up?"

He was like, "Damien, you are trying to play Call of Duty on the PlayStation 3?"

Damien was like, "Bryant let one of his homeboys hold the game without asking if it was cool."

Kevin was like, "That shit not right," so Damien said, "I have been playing the Xbox 360."

Kevin was like, "Where you get an Xbox 360 from?" so Damien was like, "It's Q's game. He got Call of Duty: Modern Warfare. You trying to play the game?"

He said, "Yeah," so I was not going to cook dinner that day because I was going to prepare Tonya's Mother's Day dinner the next day, so I decided that I was going to order pizza for everyone. I ordered four extra-large pizza from Pizza Boli's, so everybody ate and was good. I gathered the trash and threw it in the dumpster and went back into to the house. A couple of minutes later, gunshots rang off, and nobody was even scared. It was in the projects. It was normal to hear gunshots every night or every other night. I didn't give a fuck. As long as my family was good, that's all that mattered to me. Now if my family was not, then we got a problem. I am not the type that worries about what other people do. What they do does not concern me. I mind my business; I stay in my own lane. When people step foot in my lane is when it becomes a problem, so that means if you are trying to cause problems for me or my family, then I am going to deal with you accordingly to how you want to carry. If you want to fight, we can fight. You want to play with them guns, we can do that too. As a man, I am going to protect my family by all means necessary, so when I got back into the house, I started to prep the food for tomorrow so that would be one less thing I had to do for that day. After I was done with that, I went upstairs to me and Tonya's room. Her and Chantelle were in there watching one of them reality TV shows, so I left the room and let them enjoy their TV show.

I went in Damien's room. Him and Kevin were playing Call of Duty, so I watched them play the game, then Damien put that NBA 2K and challenged Kevin. He beat the hell out of Kevin. Damien picked Miami Heat; Kevin picked the Spurs. Damien beat him by thirty points, so I said, "You going to bully Kevin on the game because he doesn't know how to play, really? So you are going to use him as practice? Get nicer."

He burst out laughing. I said, "Do that now that I am on the controller."

Kevin was like, "I am nice in UFC," so I said, "Damien, pick your team."

He picked the Miami Heat again. I said okay. I picked the Boston Celtics. I destroyed the Heat, so after I beat him, Nate was there to pick Chantelle and Kevin up. Nate is Kevin's best friend. They were like brothers. Now Nate was nice with drawing, and he was nice with doing tattoos. He also very intelligent. You know how they say some of the smartest people do some of the dumbest things? That's how Nate was intelligent but would do some of the dumbest shit. He had his license, so Kevin's mother would allow him to drive her car to carry Chantelle or Kevin anywhere they wanted to go. She trusted Nate with her car. She looked at Nate as if he was her blood son, like she gave birth to him. Nate picked them up, so Chantelle gave me, her mother, and Damien a hug and said she loved us.

Kevin said, "See you all later." So after they left, I went in the room with Tonya and went to sleep. When I woke up the next morning, Tonya was getting dressed to go to church. I gave her the cards to give to her mother at church. I got up and got in the shower and washed up, brushed my teeth, and got dressed. When I came out the bathroom, Tonya was looking good and smelling good. I grabbed her on her booty.

I said, "Damn, baby, you are wearing that dress." She started laughing.

I said, "You are beautiful, baby," and gave her a kiss and a hug. I walked Tonya to the 21 bus to make sure she got on the bus safe. When the bus was coming down the street, I gave her a hug and a kiss and told her I loved her. I told her to call me when she made it to the church. She said she would. After she got on the bus, I went back into the house and went upstairs into me and Tonya's room. I watched TV.

Bryant and Jamal came home sometime that night. Now Jamal was still pissed about his phone. He knew Bryant had his phone. Tonya called me when she made it to the church. Now Tonya was getting out of church around about 12:00 p.m. to 1:00 p.m., so around 10:00 a.m., I went downstairs and put the smoked turkey necks on to cook. I seasoned my smoked turkey necks before I put them in the water. While I was cooking the string beans, I could hear somebody was walking upstairs. I could hear the person running the bathroom sink water, then that person made their way downstairs. It was Damien. He said, "Q, what up?"

I said, "What up, Damien?" He made some cereal. He asked me after I get finished cooking today, did I want to play NBA 2K? I said after I get done, he can lose. He said he was getting nicer.

I said, "Yeah, you are getting nicer," so he said, "It's only a matter of time before I get my first win."

I said, "Keep hope alive."

He burst out laughing. He said, "I am serious. Q, you got to think about when we first started playing NBA 2K. You was winning by thirty to forty points. Now when you play against me, you be winning by three points, six points. It's only a matter of time before I get that big win."

I said, "Everybody got to have a dream, but that doesn't mean it comes to reality. Keep hope alive and maybe one day, when I am an old man, you will be able to get a win, but until then, you are going to keep taking these losses."

After me and Damien were done talking trash, we heard Jamal say, "Bryant, give me my phone. I know you got my phone."

Bryant said, "Bitch-ass nigga, I don't have your phone."

Jamal said, "Your broke ass got to steal my phone? You can't buy your own phone?"

Bryant said, "You fucking gay-ass bitch! You a bitch. I got your phone, bitch-ass nigga. What are you going to do?"

Jamal said, "I am going in your room, bitch, and I am getting my phone."

Bryant said, "You go in my room, I am going to beat the shit out of you."

Jamal tried to go in his room. All you heard after that was punches being thrown. Me and Damien were downstairs, but we knew they were fighting in the hallway. The next thing you could hear was Jamal saying, "Get off me!"

Now after Bryant let him go, he said, "Bitch, this is my phone," and he came downstairs with the phone and placed the phone in the living room window. Jamal came downstairs behind him, saying, "Give me my phone, you bitch-ass motherfucker."

Bryant was like, "The phone is on the window ledge."

When Jamal tried to go and reach for the phone, Bryant punched him so hard to the point he fell back into the closet, then he walked over there and punched him three more times to the point Jamal hit the floor. Now Jamal is about 6'1" in height, and Bryant was about 5'6", and little brother beat up big bro. He beat the shit out of Jamal. After Jamal was done getting his ass whipped, he ran upstairs and said, "I am going to call the police." Damien was sitting in the living room next to the window, so Bryant said, "What you got to say?" Before Damien could say anything, he walked up to him and punched Damien so hard in the face his head went back into to the glass window and shattered the front window.

I said to Bryant, "What the fuck is wrong with you?"

There was glass everywhere, so Jamal yelled downstairs, "Q, call the police." I yelled back upstairs to Jamal and said, "Where I am from, we don't call the police for nothing. We don't believe in calling the police for anything. You have issue or a problem with a person, you handle it yourself."

But Jamal said he was about to call the police, and he did call them, so I told Bryant, "Boy, you better get out of here. You hear him on the phone with them people," so before he left, he said, "Could you make sure nobody goes in my room?" so he left.

After Bryant left, the police shortly arrived. I went upstairs. I didn't want nothing to do with them people, but I could hear Jamal telling the police that Bryant stole his phone and beat him up. They asked for his brother's full name and date of birth. He told them everything.

I said to myself, *This man is cold. He's telling them everything.* They asked him what happened to the front window.

He said, "He punched my little brother in the head so hard to the point his head went back and shattered the front window."

The police officer asked Damien if he could see the top of his head. Damien was blessed that he just had a couple of scratches because the way his head hit the window, he could have seriously gotten hurt. The officer took pictures of the window as well as the top of Damien's head. I could hear the police officer say that he was going back to his office to issue a warrant for Bryant's arrest. After the police officer left, I went back downstairs to finish cooking. Jamal asked if he could use my phone to call his mother.

I said, "Yeah, the phone is upstairs on the charger."

Before I went upstairs, I had added my string beans to the pot with the smoked turkey necks. I asked Damien if he was good. He said he was cool, so I went in the kitchen and made up my home-made macaroni and cheese. When I was done putting everything together, I put it in the oven. After that was in the oven, I mixed up the crab meat. I added my seasoning and my other ingredients. Once I was done with it, I put another pot on the stove and added the grease so I could start cooking the crab cakes. Even though Satan was busy that day, I said to myself, *Satan is a liar. Satan is not going to stop me from preparing the Mother's Day meal for my woman.* As I am cooking, I could hear Jamal up there telling his mother what happened.

It had begun to rain outside, so Tonya was on her way home, her and her niece Jessie. Everything was about done. I had fried the crab cakes, my macaroni and cheese was about done, as well as my string beans, so I ran upstairs to get something out my room. Then I noticed that Bryant's room door was open and Jamal and Damien had gone in the room and taken what they wanted, or should I say took the shit back that he had stolen from them, so I said to myself, *Oh well.* After I got what I needed, I went back downstairs and got my macaroni out the oven. I could hear somebody unlocking the door. It was Keith. He said, "What's up?"

I said, "What's up," so he looked at the window and was like damn, it was like a brawl in there. Damien came downstairs and Keith was like, "Damien, let me see your head. You blessed not to have to get no stitches."

Jamal came downstairs and told Keith everything that happened. Next thing you know, you hear the keys turning again. It was Tonya and her niece Jessie. You could tell Tonya was pissed off. She was red. She came through the door like he got to get the fuck out her house, talking about Bryant. She asked Damien if he was good.

He said yeah, he was good, so then Chantelle was calling her mother's phone to see what was going on.

Jamal ended up telling her what happened, so she said she was on her way over there. Tonya ended up calling Bryant on his phone and telling him he got to go and she wanted her key back. He said he would be there that night to get his stuff. Tonya asked how she was going to cover the window.

I said, "My grandmother has pieces of plywood that I could put at the window until maintenance comes to fix the window," so I called my grandmother to see if she still had the plywood. She said yes, she still had it. I asked her if I could get a piece of it. She said it was okay, so me and Keith and Damien drove over my grandmother's house, and we went ahead and got the plywood.

We drove back to the house, and when we walked back into the house, Chantelle and Kevin were there, so what I did was I broke a piece of plywood off where it could fit the window, then I took the screwdriver and screwed the screws in to the wall of the window to the point that the plywood could not be moved from the inside of the house as well as the outside of the house. After I was done fixing the window, I fixed me and Tonya something to eat because when she first got in the house, she didn't want to eat. That's how pissed she was. Everybody else had eaten. We were the last to eat. Everybody who ate said the food was delicious, so we ate our food.

Jessie came downstairs from upstairs in the room with Jamal, so she said, "Auntie, I am going to get a plate to go." Tonya said, "Fix Glen a plate too," so after Jessie was done fixing the plates, she went and caught the 21 bus and went home. After me and Tonya were done eating, you could hear the front door being unlocked. It was Bryant and his mentor.

Bryant went upstairs and came back downstairs and was like, "Q, I thought you was going to keep them out my room. They were in my room." I just stared at that man, so he went back upstairs, and Chantelle followed him.

All you could hear her say was, "You don't know him." That dude was mad, but how the fuck you going to get mad for someone stealing your things when you stole their shit first? It was fair game.

You stole their shit, so they came back and stole something of yours. The energy that you put in the world is going to come back to you whether it is negative or positive, and what I mean by that is if you are in the street robbing people, it is only a matter of time before someone tries to rob you or tries to kill you. I am going to give you another example. If you are out here in these streets killing people, it's only a matter of time before someone's going to kill you or try to kill you. That's why I don't understand people who do dirt, and when the same dirt that person does catches up with them, they don't understand why it happened to them. It is simple—what goes around surely comes back around.

After Bryant was done getting his stuff from upstairs, he came downstairs. Tonya asked him for her key to the house. He said Chantelle had the key. She said to get the hell out her house. As he was going out the house, he said, "Fuck you, bitch" to his mother and slammed the front door.

She said, "That bitch is disrespectful."

Tonya was pissed off even more, so I told her to calm down and not allow Satan to destroy her day, so after I got Tonya calmed down, Chantelle and Kevin asked if Keith could take them home. He said he would. After Keith took Chantelle and Kevin home, I called my baby mother's phone and talk to my daughter. I told my baby mother to drop my daughter off that Friday coming up. She said okay. After I finished talking to my daughter and my baby mother, I got my clothes ready for work the next day. Tonya had calmed down a lot now.

When I was done getting my clothes together, I lay down right next to Tonya. Next thing we know, out of nowhere, Damien burst in the room talking about "no shut doors."

I said, "You know what, little man, I got you," so me and Tonya said, "Get the hell out."

Tonya told Damien he should be getting ready for school tomorrow, so he walked out the room saying, "No shut doors," so I said to myself, *Again how in the hell does every room in this house have a lock on the door except me and Tonya's room.* I said to myself the next day after I get off work, I was going to the store and buy a lock for the door. So I went to sleep and woke up the next morning and went in brushed my teeth, washed my face, and gave Tonya a kiss. I told her I loved her and would see her later. I went and caught the 21 to the 36. I was going to the warehouse over by Washington Boulevard and unload two sugar trucks.

When I got there, I started to work on the first truck. I unloaded it and went to the next truck. My mother called to check up on me, so we talked for about ten to fifteen minutes. I asked her if she was good and did she need anything?

She said she was good and didn't need anything. I told her I loved her and would call her after I got home, so I started the second truck around about 12:00 p.m., so I was done around about 2:00 p.m. I went in the bathroom and washed up and put deodorant and a new shirt on. As I was leaving, I got a call from Tonya. She asked me if I was good. I said, yeah, Was she good? She said yeah. I said I was on my way home.

She said, "Damn, you did them two trucks that fast?"

I said, "Come on, baby, you know me. I am not going to be here all day on two trucks." So I told her I was going to the house and wash clothes as well as put in an application for Target working the night shift. She said okay. I told her I loved her and would see her when she got home. I went and caught the 36 to the 21.

When I got home, I went and got into the shower, and when I got out, I gathered all the clothes and washed them. While the clothes were washing, I went on the Target website on my phone. I clicked on "career" and filled out application for the Target out there in Cambridge. The 35 would take me straight to the job. They had shifts for the daytime and shifts for the nighttime. The daytime shift was making like $10 an hour to, like $10.50 an hour, And the night shift made $11 to $11.50 an hour. I had a daytime job, so I put in an application for the nighttime shift stocking shelves and unloading the truck as well, so after I was done filling out the application, I got the clothes out the washing machine.

I could hear the door being unlocked. It was Damien coming home from school. I asked him how school was. He said good. He was talking about his PlayStation 3 and how now that Bryant moved out, he wouldn't see his PlayStation 3 no more, the one that Bryant let his homeboy use and said he would bring the game back on Monday. "But you know he not now," so I said, "Since you been doing good in school as well as home, I am going to buy you another PlayStation 3."

He said, "Okay, cool."

I said, "I am going to buy the game this Friday." I had forgotten to go to the store when I got off, so I said to myself when I got off work the next day, I would go to the store and buy a lock for me and Tonya's room.

About thirty minutes later, I could hear Tonya turning the lock to the door. She came into the house, and I asked her how her day was. She said it was good. She said she had to make a trip up to social service before they closed, so she had to leave the day care center early. She had to take some papers up there. She said she got everything straight though, so she asked Damien how his day in school was. He said it was good. She had a big bag that had them damn boxed lunches, so Damien was like, "Q, you trying to play NBA 2K?"

I said, "Yeah, let me finish hanging up the rest of the clothes."

He said okay, so when I finished, we played the game. I won both games by like two points, so after we were done playing NBA 2K, we played Madden. He won two games, I won one game, so we played Call of Duty: Modern Warfare survival mode. After we were done playing the game, I went in the room with Tonya. We watched TV and then I fell asleep.

I woke up in the morning, washed my face, and brushed my teeth, so when I went in me and Tonya's room, she was up watching the *Jeffersons* TV show while ironing her clothes for that day. I got dressed. After I was done, I gave Tonya a kiss and a hug, and I squeezed her booty and told her I loved her and that I would see her later. She said she loved me too and for me to have a good day. So when I left the house, I went and caught the 21 to the 35 bus stop. I was going over OST warehouse. I had a black pepper truck to unload.

When I had arrived at the warehouse, the truck was not in the door. I had to wait for the yard jockey to bring the truck to door number 8 so I could unload the truck. A yard jockey is responsible for bringing all the truck to the door not just for the people who are unloading them, but he is also responsible for bringing the truck to the door for the forklift operators so that they also can unload their trucks with the forklift because their trucks have items that sometimes already comes on the pallet. The yard jockey is also responsible for when the container is empty, to remove the container from the door, so when Ron brought the truck to the door, I started unloading the truck. I was done before lunchtime, so when I was done unloading, I swept the truck out and then I went into the bathroom and tried to wash some of that black pepper smell off me. After I was done, I put another shirt on and another pair of hoop shorts.

Now OST is one of the dirtiest warehouse. The Overflow warehouses are pretty clean, so after I was done getting myself together to leave the warehouse and go catch the 35, I hollered at Mama and made sure she was good. She said she was okay, so I left and caught the 35. While I was waiting on the 35, I called my grandmother to make sure she was good and if she needed me to do anything. She said yeah, she needed me to come play her numbers and get her some scratch-offs, so I said I would be there. I could see the bus was making its way down the street, so I told my grandmother I was on my way. She said okay, so when I got off the 35 bus, I walked up the street toward Greenmount and down Biddle Street and knocked on my grandmother's door. She opened the door, so I went in the house. She had her lottery numbers ready. She said she wanted them played for midday and evening for tomorrow and the next day. Now she had scratch-offs that were winners that she had brought the day before, so she said she wanted about five scratch-offs, so after I got everything I needed to go play her number, I left out the house and went up to Phil's, which is the corner store up on Greenmount. It used to be called Kim's. Phil was his brother, so Kim started that corner store and when he made enough money, he went and invested in another store and left that store to his brother. One thing I have seen is that Mexicans as well as Chinese people support each other. I have seen with my own eyes the unity that they have for each other. I had seen Kim open that corner store up, make his money to be able to branch out, and open another corner store in a different part of the city, but he did not close it down. He said, "I am going to keep this store in the family," and he passed it down to his brother. I hear people say, "These foreigners coming over here and taking all the jobs. They got three and four different stores." That's because they work together. I watched this Mexican named Warren who worked at my job start his own landscaping business as well as working on unloading trucks. He sent a lot of money back home to his family to the point they were able to build a house in Mexico from the ground up. The things that we as black people take for granted, the next person will appreciate. You got to think a lot of these foreign countries go through poverty; they have nothing. They may be working for next to nothing, less than minimum wage, so when they get in the United States, where there's more opportunity to make money or just do anything, they do so because the wages are better than making $5 or $4 a day. That's why these foreigners are grateful, because they know how it is to be damn near starving to the point of not have anything. That's why they always support their own race. That's why they work together with each other, no hating on each other, not being envious of each other. Us as black people, we never support each other or work together. It's rare to see us supporting each other's business, but we do a lot of tearing each other down, hating on each other, or being envious of each other. I am from a city where I have seen a lot of this. Every time someone's about to make it out my city, they end up dead. It's rare we got a few stars that made it out, but that rarely happened. I'm from a city called "Body-More, Murder Land," and the name means just what it means, "body-more murder land." We are a small city, but we are one of the most violent in the world. There is a lot of envy and hatred here. We are also known as the city of crabs. You ever seen a bushel of crabs all together, and that one crab almost made it out the basket and the other crabs pull the crab back in? That's how my city is. Brothers setting their own family up for the money. In my city, you cannot let too many people know you getting money. It is the people you be around every day, the people that you trust the most, that will cause you the most pain and will bring tears to your eyes. That's real talk. Those are the ones you have to look at twice because those be the ones that that will put the knife in your back first. You ever heard the saying a stranger will treat you better than your flesh and blood? That's how it is from my side of town, East Baltimore. We got the reputation of being one of the crudest sides in Baltimore because brothers be killing brothers they grew up with like it's nothing and will attend the funeral like a brother didn't have anything to do with it. My city is a cold and heartless city.

After I got my grandmother scratch-offs and played her lottery for tomorrow and the next day, I walked back down to my grand-mother's house, and we talked for about a half hour, then I told her I loved her and to call me if she needed anything. She said she loved me too and for me to be safe. I said, "You too," so I walked up the street going toward West Baltimore, so when I got to the light rail, I walked to the Rite Aid and got a lock for me and Tonya's room door.

When I got home, no one was there, so I took the doorknob off and put the new door lock on our door. The lock came with two keys, one for me and one for Tonya, so after I was done putting the lock on the door, I gathered all the clothes. After I put the clothes in the washing machine, I went upstairs and took a shower. When I got out the shower, I got dressed and went in me and Tonya's room. I could hear the front door being unlocked. It was Tonya. She yelled upstairs, "Baby!"

I said, "Yeah?"

She said to come and help her with the bags, so I came down-stairs and brought all the bags into the house. We put the food away, so I asked her, "Baby, where everybody at?"

She said, "Damien is over one of his friend's house, and Jamal and Ronald is over Glen's house," so I said, "We got the house all to ourselves. It's time to go upstairs and spend some quality time together," so after me and Tonya got done putting the food away, we went upstairs. She noticed that the door to our room had a lock on it, so she said, "Just what we needed. Now Damien is not going to be able to burst in our room no more," so we went in our room.

I started kissing and sucking on her neck as well as nibbling on her ear. Tonya began to remove her clothes, and I began kissing on her body, sucking on her breast. I made my way down to her pussy. I loved every part of Tonya. I started kissing her inner thighs and around her pussy, then I started sucking that pussy. My tongue started to massage the clitoris. I could see that my tongue was massaging the right spot because Tonya's legs started to shake. She started to moan even louder, and she was yelling, "Daddy, that's the spot, Daddy! That's the spot right there." She started grab the sheets. I was tongue massaging that pussy, I noticed the clitoris started to get bigger and noticed Tonya's moans got even louder. She lifted her body up and looked down at me and said, "Baby, I can't stop coming, I can't stop coming."

I was hitting her spot. Her legs began to shake even more when I sucked on the clitoris of that pussy. She went crazy to the point she started to bang on the bed. She yelled, "I love you, Daddy. I love you so much, Daddy."

I noticed her clitoris began to get smaller because she was done having her orgasm. Tonya's pussy was soaking wet. She had this thick white cum coming out her pussy, so after I was done eating that pussy, I said, "Baby, I am ready to dive in that pussy. I am ready to swim in that pussy," but Tonya said, "Baby, I am tired" and to give her a minute to get herself together to take a nap.

I said to myself, *Ain't this a son of a bitch.* I was happy and sad at the same time. I was happy that Tonya got her orgasm. Now a brother was upset because she left a brother with blue balls, and I could see that her pussy was extra wet. I was so upset while Tonya was asleep. I just stared and said, "Ain't this a bitch." Tonya was sleeping good too. I could see that Tonya coming took a lot out of her. She was snoring.

Ain't that a bitch, I said to myself. *Damn.* So after I was done staring at Tonya while she was snoring, I took my upset blue balls ass in the bathroom and washed my face and brushed my teeth.

I went in Damien's room and played NBA 2K as well as a couple of games of Madden and Call of Duty: Modern Warfare survival mode, so after I was done playing the game, I went downstairs and cooked dinner. I made fried fish, corn on the cob as well as some brown rice. When I was done cooking, I took Tonya her plate. She was still sleeping, so I woke her, and she ate her food.

I said, "Damn, baby, you was knocked out."

She said, "Yeah, I know, baby. I was tired after that major orgasm." She said it took a lot out of her to the point she had to build her energy. I burst out laughing.

I said, "It took a lot out you, baby. I could tell. You went right out. You left me on blue balls state. I was ready to dive in that pussy and swim."

She burst out laughing. We ate our dinner and watched TV, so me and Tonya could hear the front door being unlocked. It was Damien, so I locked the door to show him that he could not burst in me and his mother's room no longer, so me and Tonya anxiously waited on Damien to come upstairs. This shit was about to be hilarious. Me and Tonya started to laugh. We could hear Damien coming upstairs. We knew he was going to come straight to our room. A knock on the door and he said, "Oh, now you all got a lock on your door. No locks! Open the door!"

Me and Tonya burst out laughing, so I opened the door. I said, "Yeah, little brother, you just thought you was going to be able to bust into the room?"

He said, "No locked doors," so Tonya burst out laughing. He asked me when I got the lock in, when I put the lock on the door.

I said today.

He said, "No, you all can have no lock on. The door must remain open at all times."

Me and Tonya said at the same time, "Brother, we are grown," so that brother got quiet, so Tonya asked how his day in school was. He said he had a good day. She asked if he had any homework. He said yes. I told him that Friday when I got off of work, I would order him a PlayStation 3 from Amazon. He said okay. He asked after he finished his homework, did I want to play NBA 2K?

I said, "Yeah, you can lose."

He said, "No, I am going to win this game."

I said, "Okay, I hear you. Keep hope alive because that's not going to happen," so he went and started doing his homework, and me and Tonya continued to watch TV, so after Damien was done with his homework, I went in his room and played him in a couple of games of NBA 2K. I could tell that he got even nicer since the last time we played the game. He still lost, but he got nicer, so after I was done playing the game, I went in me and Tonya's room and got my clothes ready for work the next day. Me and Tonya watched a little more TV, then I went to sleep.

I woke up the next morning. You know, the same routine—brushed my teeth, washed my face, got dressed, gave Tonya a hug and a kiss, and I caught the 21 to the 36 bus. I was going to the Overflow warehouse on Washington Boulevard to unload a truck that contained fifty-pound bags of sugar as well as a truck that contained glass jars of sauerkraut. When I arrived at the sugar warehouse, I started working on the sugar truck first. I unloaded the truck by 11:30 a.m., then I started to work on the sauerkraut container. I was done with both trucks about 2:30 p.m., so when I was done, I did my same routine and went and washed up and got myself together to go and catch the bus. When I got up the street, the bus was coming down the street, so I got on.

When I arrived home, I noticed that the front window was fixed. The maintenance people had come and fixed the living room window. I could hear that Jamal was in the house. He was talking to Ronald, who was also in the house, so I went in the kitchen and fixed me something to eat left over from yesterday. I warmed my food up in the microwave. When my food was done, I went upstairs and spoke to both Jamal and Ronald, then I went to me and Tonya's room and ate my food and watched TV. After I was done eating, I gathered me and Tonya's clothes. After I put the clothes in the washing machine, I went and got in the shower. After I was done in the shower, I got dressed and got the clothes out the washing machine. I hung the clothes up around the house.

As you can see so far, my life was predictable. It was the same routine every day—go to work, come home, take care of my family. Me I don't like to be around a lot of people, so I don't go to clubs or parties. That's not my scene. I am more laid back. I go to work, come chill in the house with my family. Yeah, you can call me a boring-ass brother because I don't smoke weed or because I only drink on occasions. I am cool with being called a boring-ass brother. I have seen certain family members of mine smoke so much weed as well as cigarettes as well as pop so many pills such as oxycodone and molly to the point they gained a habit. They spent so much money on buying drugs over the years to the point they could have brought a house, car, or whatever. They became addicted to the drug of their choice. I have seen how the drugs had certain family members of mine, so I always told myself that I would not ever be like that. I have smoked weed as well as drunk liquor, but I was not addicted to it, nor did I have a habit for it.

After I was done hanging the clothes up, I went upstairs and watched TV. I could hear the front door being unlocked. It was Damien and Tonya, so Tonya called me downstairs to help with the bags. She'd gone to the market again, so me and Damien brought all the bags of food in the house. We put all the food away. I asked Tonya how her day was. She said it was okay. She asked me the same thing, how was my day. I said it was good, so after I was done talking to Tonya and Damien, I called my baby mother, and I talked to my daughter for an hour. I told her I couldn't wait to see her on Friday.

I said, "I love you, Kiwi doodle. You are my heartbeat," so after I talk to my daughter as well as her mother, I called my mother and made sure she was good. She said she was okay. She said she went over my grandmother's house and checked on her and made sure she was good. She said she went and played her number, and they sat and talked. She stayed over there for about two hours, got some more of her things from her old room.

I asked her how Cornell was doing. She said him and his daughter, Sharon, got into an argument because Cornell would come in the house all drunk, yelling, waking up the kids. He would be fussing, cursing. She said Sharon got tired of it, so they got into an argument. He called her a whole bunch of bitches. She said he was not shit.

He said, "I am your father."

She said, "You not my father! What have you done for me? You were not even a part of my life! I grew up in a fucking foster home because you were in fucking prison."

He said to her, "You not my fucking daughter!" He said he would kill her. Now Cornell had fifteen kids. Now a lot of women were saying their kids was his, and he never got the DNA test to see whether or not they were his kids or not. He just claimed all of them as his kids. Think of the worst thing your parent could say to you as well as think of the worst thing your child could say to you. Cornell and his daughter would argue and say the most disrespectful shit you could say to your parent and a parent could say to their child. Cornell had a real bad drinking problem. He had a habit when it came to drinking. He would get so drunk to the point he would blank out. He would sleep outside, and he would get into fights and would not remember how it happened or what happened. My mother said he would come in the house with scars, and she would nurse him back to health. Now when Cornell was sober, he was cool, but like anyone who has a habit, it's like whatever your drug of choice is, it be calling your name. You got to find a way to get high. Now when Cornell was sober, he would be quiet and get irritated real fast. My mother told me a lot of times when Cornell was sober, he would pick a lot of arguments just so he could use that as an excuse to go out and get drunk. For example, if my mother said the sky was blue, he would try some way to disagree with her even though it's the truth. He would turn that into some type argument so he could go out and get drunk. My mother really loved Cornell. She put up with a lot of his shit. He had a real bad drinking problem. It was bad to the point he could drink a fifth of liquor like it was water. His drinking was so bad he had cirrhosis of the liver. The doctor told him that if he didn't stop drinking, he was going to die. Cornell did not pay the doctor any mind. As soon as he got out the hospital, he went right back to drinking.

Before we got off the phone, I told her I loved her and asked what was up with my little brother Moses. She said he was good, still at my grandmother's house. After I was done talking to my mother, me and Tonya started watching TV. Damien came in the room and was like, "Q, after I finish my homework, what up with playing NBA 2K?"

I said, "You can lose a couple of games," so me and Tonya continued to watching TV. After Damien was done with his homework, we played NBA 2K. Also, we played a couple of games of Madden.

After I was done winning in the game, I went and got my clothes ready for work the next day. I called my baby mother's phone and talked to my daughter before she went to bed. I told her I loved her and would see her Friday. After I was done talking to my daughter, me and Tonya watched TV until I went to sleep and woke up the next morning.

I got up, washed my face, brushed my teeth, and got dressed. Tonya was up ironing her clothes. She went in the room and woke Damien up for school. After I was done getting dressed, I gave Tonya a hug and a kiss and went and caught the 21 bus to the 35 bus. I was going to the OST warehouse, unloading trucks of black pepper and one twenty-footer of cases of pineapple in a can.

I was done with both trucks around 3:00 p.m., so I went and washed up in the bathroom. When I was done washing up, I went and caught the 35 to the 21. When I arrived home, I got in the shower and put me and Tonya's clothes in the washing machine. I received a phone call from a number I did not recognize, but something told me to answer the phone. So I answered. and the person on the other end of the phone said, "Hello, is this a Quentin Ford?"

I said, "Yes, who is asking?"

He said, "My name is Michael, and I am a supervisor at Target. I see that you put in an application at Target for the night shift. Are you still interested in the night job stocking shelves as well as unloading the truck?"

I said, "Yeah."

He said, "Well, can you come in for an interview on Monday?"

I said, "Yes I can."

He said, "We are the Target located at 5250 Campbell Boulevard. Be there at 10:00 a.m. for the interview," so I said, "Okay, I will be there," so after I got off the phone with the supervisor for Target, I instantly looked up what bus went out there. I had seen that the 35 went right there to Target. I had two ways I could get to the 35. I could catch the 21 to Greenmount and walk down the street to the 35, or I could walk down to the light rail by the state center, and right across from the light rail was the subway, get off the subway right there by Johns Hopkins, and I would walk. Around the corner, the 35 bus stop was right there.

After I was done looking up the location of the store as well as how to get out there, I went upstairs and watched TV. I could hear the front door being unlocked. It was Damien coming home from school. I called my grandmother and checked up on her and made sure she was good and that she didn't need anything. She said she was good. I told her that I had a job interview at Target on Monday. She said, "Congratulations" because she knew God would bless me with the job.

I said, "Thanks, Grandma. I appreciate that."

She had just gotten back into the house from downtown. She said it was a beautiful day out, so she'd taken a trip downtown. When it's warm outside, my grandmother stayed on the go. She was catching all the sales at the markets. She was taking trips to the casino. My grandmother's the only person I know that if it's a 120 degrees outside, she would be in the house with no air conditioner or fan on. She would not break a drop of sweat.

While I was talking to my grandmother, I could hear the front door being opened and could hear Tonya yelling, "Hello? Is anybody home?" After I was done talking to my grandmother, I told her I loved her. She said the same, so when I hung up the phone, I went downstairs and gave Tonya a hug and kiss and told her I loved her. I could see that she'd brought home some more of them damned school lunch boxes. I asked her how her day was. She said it was good. I told her I got an interview at Target. She said, "Congratulations, baby."

I said, "Thank you. I will be working the night shift when I get the job." I was speaking it into existence, so she said, "Baby, I know you going to get the job because you are a hard worker, and hard work pays off." She asked me if I knew how to get to the job.

I said, "Yeah, I already looked up how to get there. I am just waiting on Monday."

She asked what I was going to wear. I said, "I am going to get a button-up shirt as well as some khakis and some Jordans. They did not say I had to dress up, just wear causal clothes. After I get off work tomorrow, I am going to go get me a pair of khakis. I already got a shirt to wear. I am just going to get the pants. That way I can be ready for Monday." Little did I know, next week was going to be a crazy week.

So after I was done talking to Tonya, I went back upstairs and got my stuff ready for work the next day. After getting my clothes together, I was talking to Tonya when my baby mother called my phone and asked what time I wanted her to drop Kiwi off.

I said, "Around 4:00 p.m. the next day."

She said okay. I said, "I got an interview at Target."

She said congratulations.

I said, "Thank you."

She asked what I was going to do about the other job.

I said, "I am going to work both jobs. I am going to work Target at nighttime, and I am going to work at the Overflow warehouse during the day. I said I don't have to be at work at Target until 11:00 p.m., and I get off work at 7:00 a.m., so when I leave work at Target in the morning, I would go to whatever warehouse I had to work at that day, I would do two trucks and be done around 3:00 p.m. then go home and take a shower, wash clothes, and go to sleep. I got it all planned out.

She said I was going to be tired as hell.

I said, "I am about to get this money. Now all I need to do is make it through the interview, which Lord's will, I already got the job."

She said, "You got the job."

I told her to put my Kiwi Doodle on the phone, so I could tell her I couldn't wait to see her, so she put her on the phone.

I said, "Kiwi doodle, I love you. I miss you."

She said, "I love you too, Daddy, and I miss you."

I said, "I love you. Have a good night's sleep. Let me speak to your mother." I said, "I will see you tomorrow."

When I got off the phone, I called Damien in the room. I told him tomorrow when I got off work, I was going to put the money on my Bank of America card, and when he got home from school, we could order him another PlayStation 3.

I said, "Is there a game you want to play on the system?"

He said, "Yeah, NBA 2K."

I said okay, so after I was done talking to Damien, I went to sleep so I could get up for work the next day. Now that next Wednesday was my birthday, June 6. I was turning the age of twenty-four, but I looked at birthdays as just another day in another year that God has blessed me to see. I was turning twenty-four, which was a blessing in itself because in my city, a lot of brothers were not making it to twenty, so when you made it to the age twenty-four to thirty, you were blessed.

I woke up the next morning and did the same routine—washed my face, brushed my teeth, and got dressed, but before I left, I gave Tonya a hug and a kiss and told her I loved her and I'd see her later. I went and caught the 21 to the 36. I was going over to the warehouse on Washington Boulevard to unload two sugar trucks. Pat had told me he would drop my money off to me at the warehouse. Troy was working at the furniture warehouse, so when I arrived, I started on my first truck about 11:30 a.m. It was 1:00 p.m. when I finished my first truck. Pat was walking through the warehouse door, so he said, "Q, come sign your receipt for your money," so I signed the receipt, and he gave me an envelope that had my money.

I said, "Pat, I got a job interview on Monday at Target, so I am going to take that day off." He said okay, so after I was done talking to Pat, I started the next truck. I finished the truck at 2:30 p.m. When I finished, I went in the bathroom and washed up and put some deodorant on and a new shirt. I caught the bus and went downtown to the Bank of America. I went to the ATM, and I put the money for Damien's game in the bank, plus the money for NBA 2K, so after I was done, I went in to DTLR, which means Downtown Locker Room. I went in there and got me some khakis for my interview on Monday, plus I grabbed my daughter two pairs of Jordans. After I paid for the stuff and left DTLR, I caught the light rail up to the culture center and then I walked through the projects until I got to my house.

When I got in the house, I got in the shower and washed some clothes. Nobody was home. I watched a little TV until the washing machine stopped, then I hung up the clothes outside on the line.

When I was done hanging the clothes, I went back into the house. I could hear the front door being unlocked. It was Jamal and Ronald. They said, "What's up?"

I said, "What up?"

Jamal asked if his mother was home. I said, "No, she did not get home yet," so him and Ronald went upstairs. Tonya called my phone and asked me if I could go to the corner store and get her a pack of cigarettes, a Pepsi, some chips, and sunflower seeds. I said, "Okay, I got you," so I walked down the street to the corner store.

When I got back to the house, Damien was home from school. I asked him if he was ready to order his game. He said yeah. I told him to ask Jamal if he could use his laptop so he could order his game. Jamal said yes, he could use the computer. Now we had Wi-Fi through DirecTV. It was Verizon Internet, but it was not good-quality Internet. I was going to get Comcast cable as well as their Internet, but Comcast had put a red flag on the house, meaning the people who had lived here before us must have gotten service with Comcast and did not pay their bill. Comcast put in their computer that the house was a red flag. Before I got DirecTV in my name, Tonya had called Comcast to get their cable at the house, but they said they would need her lease stating that she just moved in the house. They needed a copy of her social security card as well as her birth certificate, so Tonya asked what I wanted to do. I said, "Baby, don't worry about it. Them people act like they are trying to do a background check for a job. All we are trying to do is get some cable and Internet."

So I said, "Tonya, baby, I am going to get DirecTV for the house." It just so happened that through DirecTV, we were able to get Verizon Internet, but it was not Fios Verizon, which is a better Internet service. I called Verizon to see if we would be able to get it in our area. They said they did not provide Internet service here, which is the projects; they provided Internet service out in the county. So I just got the Internet through DirecTV, which was much slower.

Me and Damien were looking for PlayStation 3s on Amazon. I ordered him a "used, like new" PlayStation 3 from Amazon as well as an NBA 2K with another controller. I placed the order. It would be there on that Monday. After I was done ordering the game, my baby mother called my phone and said she was on the way to drop our daughter off. I said okay. After I got off the phone, I started cooking dinner. I was making fried fish, corn on the cob, Brussels sprouts.

While I was cooking, I heard a knock at the door. I went and opened the door. It was my baby mother and my daughter. Before I could say, "Kiwi doodle!" she said, "Daddy!" and ran to me. I picked her up and gave her a whole bunch of kisses and told her I loved her and I missed her. My baby mother gave me a bag with Kiwi's things. She had a ride. Her sister Tiara had brought her to the house, so after I got Kiwi's things, her mother went and got back into the car. I shut the door and asked my Kiwi doodle if she was hungry. She said yes, so I made her a plate, put a towel on the floor, and sat her food on the floor. She sat down and ate her food. While she was eating, I could hear Tonya coming through the front door.

She said, "Hello, Kiwi. Hello, baby. How was your day?"

I said, "Good." I asked her the same question. She said she had a good day too, then she asked, "When did Kiwi get here?"

I said a few minutes before she came into the house, so she said, "Damien got in yet?"

I said, "Yeah, he upstairs," so she made her a plate and went upstairs, but before she went upstairs, I gave her the stuff she asked me to get her from the store.

She said, "Okay, thank you," so after I took the last pieces of fish out the grease, me and Kiwi went upstairs. Tonya was in Jamal's room smoking. Damien was playing the Xbox. Me and Kiwi doodle went in the room and watched TV. Damien came in the room and asked if I was trying to play the game. I said, "Yeah, I will play," so I put cartoons on for Kiwi, and I went and played the game. When I was done, I ran my daughter's bathwater, washed her up, and got her dressed and ready for bed. After I got my daughter ready for bed, me and Tonya watched TV until she went to sleep, then I turned the channel to the sports channel. I stayed until six in the morning, then I went to sleep. I woke up around about 1:00 p.m. Kiwi and Tonya were already awake. Ronald had made breakfast for everyone in the house. Now Ronald was gay. He'd finished college. Also, he was a chef. He could cook. Ronald was forty-nine or fifty years old. He was

Jamal's slave. Whatever Jamal said, he would do. If Jamal said jump, he would say, "How high you want me to jump?" It's to the point where one day, Ronald was sleep and Jamal was hungry. He woke Ronald up and told him to go fix him something to eat. Anytime Jamal said he was hungry, Ronald would ask him, "What do you want to eat?" and go fix it. If Jamal say he wanted some weed, Ronald would make a way and get the weed for him. He was treated like shit. Now Ronald he was an alcoholic. He would get drunk and not know what to say out his mouth. For that he got a lot of ass whippings by different people, Jessie being one of them people. Now it was told to me at one point in Ronald's life, he had money and took good care of Jamal, buying him cars, clothes, everything Jamal wanted, but he lost all the money he had. It's crazy. He started off with everything— house, cars, money—and lost it all to the point he was reduced to sleeping on Tonya's dining room floor. God can give you everything, but he can also take everything from you, and that's what happened to Ronald. I noticed when people think they are better than other people who are less fortunate than them, God takes everything from that person and puts them at a level that is less than the person they thought they were better than. It's crazy 'cause that person that was less fortunate ends up helping that same person who looked at them as less of a person. That's how God works. You can take everything for granted, and he will take it all away no matter how much money you have.

Now I got up, washed my face, brushed my teeth, went and got my breakfast out the microwave, and ate. Chantelle was bringing Mama over that day, so she could play with Kiwi. She said Mama had been asking about Kiwi, so about two hours later Chantelle and Kevin and mama knocked on the door. Damien went and unlocked the door and let them in, so everybody came upstairs. Chantelle and Kevin came in me and Tonya's room and said, "What up?"

Mama came in the room and saw Kiwi, and Kiwi saw Mama. They gave each other a hug. Mama was like, "Kiwi! Hey, Kiwi, I miss you!"

Kiwi said, "I miss you too," so two minutes later, they went downstairs and started getting into stuff in the refrigerator. I went downstairs to get something out of the refrigerator, and I saw bitten baloney on the kitchen floor. I noticed when I came downstairs, both Kiwi and Mama ran upstairs because they knew what they did was wrong, so I cleaned up the mess they made. As I was going upstairs, Mama and Kiwi were coming back downstairs. I said, "No, no, no. Turn around and go back upstairs. You all not making no more messes." So when I got upstairs, I went in me and Tonya's room. Kiwi and Mama were sitting on the bed looking innocent. Tonya and Chantelle were watching TV. I said, "Keep an eye on these two bad babies."

Tonya and Chantelle said at the same time, "Why, what happened?"

I said, "They both decided they wanted to play in the refrigerator, biting on bologna and throwing it in the floor."

Chantelle was like, "Mama, you know better."

I said, "Kiwi, you better not go back downstairs."

I went in Damien's room and played the game with Damien and Kevin. We played Call of Duty: Modern Warfare and Madden and NBA 2K. About three hours later, Kevin called Nate to come pick him and Chantelle and Mama up. They were ready to go home. Nate got there an hour later. After Chantelle, Kevin, and Mama left, I went downstairs and fixed Kiwi something to eat. After she ate her food, I prepared her bubble bath and got her ready for bed, so after my daughter went to bed I went downstairs, washed the dishes, and took out the trash. I mopped the kitchen and the dining room floor as well as the living room floor. After I was done with that I went back upstairs. Tonya was in the room watching TV, talking on the phone, so I called my baby mother and told her I would bring our daughter home tomorrow at 5:00 p.m. She said okay, so after I got off the phone with her, I watched a little TV then I went downstairs and made sure both of the doors were locked. I made sure all the windows were shut and locked. I would do this every night. You can never be too cautious. I like to stay on point at all times. You can call it being paranoid. I call it being a protector of the people I love such as my family. As a man, this is one of the principles I stand on wholeheartedly—to provide for my family by all means.

After I made sure the house was good, I went back upstairs. That brother Damien was like, "Q, did you track where the PlayStation 3 was?"

I said, "No, I just ordered it Friday. Why, did you?"

He said, "No, I did not get the computer and track where the game is at," so he got the computer and looked it up. It said they had shipped the game off, and it would be delivered on Monday. I said, "Okay, after my interview on Monday, I will be here waiting for UPS to deliver the game."

After I was done talking to Damien, I went in me and Tonya's room. Both Tonya and my Kiwi doodle was knocked out, both of them snoring, so I watched TV until about 6:00 a.m. and then I went to sleep. I woke up around 10:30 a.m. to 11:00 a.m. I got up, washed my face, and brushed my teeth. After I was done, I went downstairs. Kiwi doodle was downstairs with Tonya. Tonya had fixed Kiwi something. I gave Kiwi doodle a hug and a kiss and told her I loved her, then I gave Tonya a kiss and a hug. I smacked her on her big booty.

She said, "I love you too, baby," so after I was done eating, I went and got in the shower. I got dressed in, then I got my daughter dressed. Tonya was like, "It's only 2:00 p.m. What, you are taking her home early?"

I said, "No, we are going over my grandmother's house. She has not seen Kiwi in weeks. After we are done, we're going to catch the light rail to Patapsco and get on the 64 bus to Brooklyn." Me and Kiwi doodle caught the 21 to my grandmother's house. When we arrived at my grandmother's house, I knocked on the door.

She said, "Who is it?"

I said, "It's your grandson."

She opened the door. She had seen Kiwi doodle, and Kiwi doodle had seen her. They gave each other a hug, and Grams said, "I miss my Kiwi doodle. I love you."

Kiwi said, "I love you too, Grandma."

My grandmother asked me to go to the store and get her some scratch-offs and to play her numbers for today and tomorrow, so after she gave me her scratch-offs and the paper with her numbers, I went up the street to Phil's and played her numbers for that day and tomorrow.

After I was done, I went back down the street. There really was not anybody on my block. It was dead around there. There were people that I knew up on Greenmount, but everybody on my block was dead or in jail with a lot of time. Some people I knew moved from around there, but a lot of the people that I grew up with were dead or in jail, so my block was like a ghost block. A lot of the houses around there, Johns Hopkins bought and was buying people who owned their house, and the ones who had their house through public housing, they were just relocating them to another house that was also public housing. They had already started knocking down houses that they brought, and the ones that were living in public housing, but there were some people who owned their house who did not sell their house until the city made them an offer they could not refuse. They didn't jump at the first offer that the city made. They were like, "No, we are going to wait and see how bad they want the house," which is smart because if they want that house bad enough for whatever they are trying to build, they are going to pay your asking price, plus relocation fees for everyone who is living in your house. A lot of people in my neighborhood waited it out, and it worked out for them. I myself should have waited it out with my house and started fixing it up. They would have not liked that because they would have to pay me more money because they not only would have had to pay me the appraisal money for the house, but if I had started to fix it up, I would have made them pay me the money that I put into the house.

Now the house my grandmother was living in, the landlord lost the house to the bank. He had put so many liens and loans against the house to the point he could not pay them back, so they just took the house. Even though they took the house, this dude still owed them more money, but my grandmother later found out that there were no leans or loans against the house; he just wanted my grandmother to move from the house because it got to the point he would not come and fix anything thing in the house, so my grandmother started paying to get things fixed in the house that he was supposed to fix. It got to the point my grandmother stopped paying him rent because he was not fixing anything, so instead of him saying. "Ms. Rose, I just want you to move," he made it so that the bank took the house. He put loans against the house and liens on the house. My grandmother was going to buy the house, and she asked me and my mother and my cousin if she should buy the house. We all told her the same thing, which was, "Hell no!" This house was not worth the price that the landlord wanted for it—$40,000 to $50,000. It was not worth that because it needed at least $50,000 to a $100,000 in repairs.

I went back into my grandmother's house. I gave her the stuff, and me and Kiwi stayed there for about two hours, chilling with my grandmother. She had given Kiwi so many snacks to the point I had to get a bag to carry all the stuff. I gave my grandmother a hug and a kiss and told her I loved her. Kiwi gave her a hug and a kiss too, but before we left, I asked her where my little brother was. She said she didn't know where he was.

"He be outside all day and come to the house all late." She said she told him if he didn't get to the house by 10:00 p.m., then she was not getting up to open the door. He would just be out there to the morning. She said she told him that her house was the house that nobody really wanted to live at because she had her rules just like anybody else. When you move into their house, they got rules and regulations that they want you to abide by, or else you can get out.

So after me and Kiwi doodle left my grandmother's house, we walked about three to four blocks up the street to the light rail. We caught the light rail to BWI airport, but we were not going to BWI. That's just where the light rail that we had to get on was, so we got on the light rail and got off at Patapsco station. We got on the 64 to Brooklyn projects. When me and Kiwi got off the bus, across the street, somebody's furniture and clothes and everything was outside their house; they'd gotten evicted from their house. We looked up the street. Somebody was up there fighting. Me and Kiwi doodle walked to her mother's house. I knocked on my baby mother's house door, and her mother opened the door.

I said, "Hey, how you are doing?"

"I am good," she said. "Come on in," so me and Kiwi went in the house. She said, "Hey, my Kiwi doodle, you had fun with your dad?"

She said yes, so I said, "I am coming to pick her up this Friday coming," so I gave her the bag and gave Kiwi doodle a hug and a kiss and told her I loved her and I would see her on Friday. Now when I left the house, the bus was coming back down the street, so I ran to the bus and got on. I got off the bus at Patapsco and got on the light rail.

I got off the light rail at the culture center and walked across the street to the 21 bus stop. I waited for the bus for about a half hour before the bus came. I could have walked home and gotten home before the bus got there. So I got on the bus, and it dropped me off across the street from my house.

I went in the house. Tonya was downstairs on the phone. She was sitting in the dining room, going through the bags that she had in storage along with the totes she had, so I went over there and gave her a hug and a kiss and grabbed a handful of her booty while she was on the phone. She was smiling her ass off. She told the person she was on the phone with to hold on, so she put them on mute, and she said, "Baby, I want some dick." I started smiling with a big-ass smile.

I said, "Last time you went to sleep on me after I ate your pussy, and you left me with blue balls."

She said, "I know, baby. I want to make that up to you."

I said, "Sounds good to me, baby. I cannot wait! You going to have to moan quietly when I am hitting your spot, baby." We were going to have to turn on the radio, play some real loud music or something because she was going to be moaning real loud. She started smiling, and she said later that night she was ready for me to dive in that pussy.

I burst out laughing and said, "I am always ready to dive in your pussy, baby."

She burst out laughing.

I said, "Baby, you know you got that super wet pussy, baby."

She was still laughing.

I said, "I will see you upstairs later in our bedroom."

She started smiling. So after me and Tonya were done talking shit to each other, I went upstairs. As soon as I got to the top of the stairs, I hear go Damien, "Q, what up with that NBA 2K?"

I said, "Yeah, I'll play you in a couple of games." So we played two games of NBA 2K. He won a game, and I won a game. He finally got his first win. As soon as the numbers on the clock hit 00, the game was over, and that brother started talking shit. He said, "You is not going to get another win."

I said, "Okay, play another game," so when that game was over, that brother was quiet as a church mouse. That's how bad he lost the game.

After I was done playing the game with Damien, I went in to me and Tonya's room and got my clothes ready for my interview for the next day, then I watched some TV. I could hear Tonya calling me, so I went back downstairs. I could see that she had gone through all the bags in the totes. She had two bags of things that needed to be thrown into the dumpster, so I took out the trash. Now she still had three bags in two totes that contained a lot of pocketbooks. When I got back in the house from throwing the two bags of trash out, Tonya was in the kitchen washing the dishes. I walked behind her, and I gave her a hug from behind. As I was hugging her from behind, I started kissing her on her neck. I turned her around and started kissing her on her lips, and I told her I loved her.

She said, "I love you too, baby," so I smacked her on her booty and told her I would be waiting upstairs for her, so I went upstairs and got in the shower. When I got out, I got dressed and brushed my teeth. When I came out the bathroom, Tonya was getting her clothes to go into the shower. She went into the bathroom and took a shower. When she came out, she was smelling so good, so she locked the door and sat down on the bed. I got closer to her. She started smiling, so we started kissing, and I started sucking on her neck. While I was kissing and sucking on her neck, she grabbed my dick and started jerking my dick off, then she pushed me back on the bed and started giving me head. The whole time she was giving me head, she was looking me in my eyes.

I said to myself, *Damn, I love this woman*, so after she was done sucking the skin off my dick, she climbed up on the bed and started riding my dick. She was looking at me, and she started biting her bottom lip. I started holding on all that booty while she was riding me. I smacked her on her ass. I started talking shit to her and smacked her on her booty again.

I said, "Whose pussy is this?"

She said, "Yours, Daddy. It's your pussy."

That pussy was so wet. She started shaking and moaning louder, then I started sucking on her breast. I could tell that she was coming. I flipped her over on her back so I could get deeper in that good pussy. I started grinding in that pussy. I started tongue kissing her while grinding in that pussy, then I started sucking on her neck. She was moaning loudly. She had come twice. I started beating that pussy up. I had her legs up in the air. I started sucking on her toes while I was beating that pussy up. She really started going crazy. We were both sweating bullets, and it was hot as shit in the room. Now I started hitting that pussy from the back with all that booty clapping like somebody was clapping their hands. That booty was moving like a waterbed. I was grabbing her thighs. The faster I would beat it up from the back, the louder her booty would clap down. She had cum again. That pussy was so wet too. I nut all in that pussy while I was hitting it from the back. After we were done making love, we went and got into the shower, and we washed up. We got out the shower and got dressed, so after we got dressed, we brushed our teeth and then we went in our room and watched a little TV. Tonya fell asleep lying on my chest, then I cut the TV off and went to sleep myself.

We woke up the next morning, and we washed our face and brushed our teeth. I went downstairs and made breakfast for everyone—scrambled eggs with cheese. I made pancakes as well as beef scrapple. So after I made breakfast, I took Tonya her breakfast before she left to go to the day care center. She said thank you, and while she was eating, I got dressed, so I could walk her to the bus stop. After I got dressed, I told Damien and Jamal that there was breakfast downstairs. Damien was instantly, "Oh yeah, I am about to go get some breakfast."

So after Tonya was done eating, I walked her to the bus stop. Before she got on the bus, I gave her a hug and a kiss and told her I loved her and would see her later, so she said she loved me too and good luck with my interview. I said thank you. I went back into the house, and Damien was leaving the house for school, and he said, "Q, don't forget about the PlayStation being delivered today."

I said, "I got you." After I locked the door and went upstairs to me and Tonya's room, I watched a little bit of TV. After I was done watching TV, I went and got in the shower and got dressed. I was about to leave the house and go to my interview when I noticed Jamal was still home, so I asked him if he could he listen out for Damien's PlayStation. "It's going to be delivered today."

He said he would listen out for the game, so after I was done talking to Jamal about the game, I walked to the subway and I got off the subway at Johns Hopkins. I caught the 35 bus to Target. When I arrived, I had to go through two interviews. At the first interview, they were asking me questions, like how did I hear about the job, as well as have I ever worked for Target?

I said no and said I went on the Target website and put in an application for the night shift. He asked me if I have ever unloaded truck. I said, "Yeah, I work at Overflow unloading trucks.

He said, "Name a time that you had to work with someone else to get the job done."

I used the story about the time me and Troy worked together to unload six trucks in one day. I said, "When we left the job that day to go home, every truck in the door was an empty container."

He asked why they should hire me. I said, "If you hire me, you would be hiring a man that is going to be reliable, who is a hard worker, who is going to come to work every day on time and do his job."

I could see I was about to get the job because I was answering each question right and with an honest answer. After I was done, he left out the room, and when he came back into the room, he was with a white lady. She was carrying a folder, and they said congratulations, I got the job.

In the folder she had papers that went over the salary that the job paid. She said the job would be paying $11.50 an hour. I would be working at nights. She said the shift would start after the store closed, which was at 10:00 p.m. to 7:00 a.m. She said sometimes they may ask if I could stay an extra hour over. She asked me if I wanted to take a drug test that day or come back tomorrow because I had to come back for orientation the next day anyway, so I said I would take the drug test that day, so she said okay. I had to wait about fifteen to twenty minutes, and the lady brought a lab cup for urine. I went in to the bathroom and pissed in the cup. When I was done, I washed my hands and wiped off the cup and put it in a plastic bag. I left the bathroom and gave the cup to the lady who does the urine test.

After I was done, I went across the street and caught the 35 going back down to Johns Hopkins. The bus stop was right across the street from Target, so I got off the 35 bus stop at Johns Hopkins and walked around the corner to the subway. I got on the subway and got off, walked up the escalator, and walked up the street to the 21 bus stop. When the bus got there, it carried me up the street to my house. I got off the bus and went in the house. I could see that Damien's game was not delivered yet. Nobody was home. Jamal had left the house, so I went upstairs and watched a little TV. I got a phone call from my grandmother asking me how the job interview went. I told her I got the job.

She said, "All right now, congratulations."

I said thank you.

She asked when I would start.

I said, "I start Thursday night."

She said, "Do you start work on your birthday?"

I said, "Yeah, on my birthday. I got to go for orientation tomorrow. They are going over everything about the job."

She asked me what I wanted for my birthday. I said, "Nothing, Ma. I am good."

She said she was going to get me something anyway. I asked how she was doing. She said she was doing good. She said she had, not too long ago, got back into the house. I asked her about my little brother. She said he, not too long ago, left out the house. I said okay. I saw that I was getting another incoming call. It was Tonya, so I told my grandmother that I would call her back and that I loved her. She said she loved me too, so I answered the phone.

Tonya said, "Baby, how did the interview go?"

I said, "Baby, I got the job."

She said congratulations. I said thank you. She said, "When do you start?"

I told her the same thing that I told my grandmother, which was I started work on Thursday night. I said, "I got to go to orientation tomorrow. They were going to go over something."

She asked me what time I got to be there.

I said, "At 10:00 a.m."

She said I got to get up early.

I said, "Yeah, I know." I told her that I would see her when she got home. I was about to call Pat and let him know that I got the job as well as that I had orientation the next day at 10:00 a.m. After I was done with orientation, I still wanted to unload a truck. Pat said congratulations.

I said, "Thank you. I am still going to work both jobs."

He asked what hours I would be working at Target. I said, "From 11:00 p.m. to 7:00 or 8:00 a.m., so after I get off work at Target, I will be going straight to whatever warehouse you send me to that day to unload the truck."

He said, "Okay, when do you start?"

I said, "Thursday night."

He said okay, and I said, "I got orientation tomorrow. That should be over around about 10:30 a.m. to 11:00 a.m."

He said since I am over there near OST, there was going to be a late truck that would arrive at 12:00 p.m., so I said okay, I would go and unload the truck.

He said, "Okay, thank you, and congratulations again."

I said thank you, so after I was done talking to Pat, I went downstairs and fixed me something to eat. After I was done, I gathered all the clothes and started washing them. While the clothes were being washed, I got my clothes ready for tomorrow. I had the clothes for orientation, plus the clothes for work when I got done with orientation at Target. I was going to go unload a truck at OST. I put them clothes in the book bag. When I got to OST, I would go in the bathroom and change into my work clothes. After I was done with getting my clothes together, I could hear somebody unlocking the front door. Al. I heard was, "Q?"

I said, "Yeah?"

He said, "Did the PlayStation 3 get here yet?"

I said, "The game is downstairs in the box."

He said, "Thank you, Q. I appreciate."

I said, "Young blood, now you can give me my Xbox 360 back so I can play NBA 2K."

He said, "Now I got to get my game collection back up."

I said, "You keep doing good in school, I will get you all the new games.

He said "already," which means "okay," so I got my Xbox. I went downstairs and I got the clothes out the washing machine. I hung the clothes up outside on the line. I went back into the house and played NBA 2K. I could hear somebody unlocking the front door. It sounded like it was Jamal and Ronald. All I know was that I heard some barking, and I could hear a dog running up the stairs. It was a shih tzu. That dog came in me and Tonya's room and then Jamal called her name, "April!" She ran back downstairs.

I called my mother to check up on her to make sure she was good. I told her I got the job at Target.

She said congratulations.

I said thank you. I said, "What's going on?"

She said, "Nothing, the same shit, just a different day."

I said, "True that. You need anything?"

She said no.

I said, "Let me know if you need anything."

She said okay. I said, "What's up with Cornell?"

She said, "He good. Sharon had put him out the house, but she let him back in the house, so he has been chilling with the drinking."

I said, "True that."

She asked how her granddaughter was doing.

I said, "She is good. I took her over to Grandma's house. They were happy to see each other."

She said, "That's what up." She said she got to get Kiwi for a weekend.

I said, "Yeah. What up with Moses? You talked to him?"

She said yeah, he'd called her through his homeboy's cell phone. I said, "True that," so before I got off the phone with my mother, I told her I loved her and to be safe, that I would talk to her later. She said she loved me more and for me to be safe as well, so after I was done talking to my mother, I heard Tonya coming through the front door. She said, "Where the fuck this dog come from?"

I burst out laughing. As she was coming in the house, the dog was barking at the door, so Jamal called the dog upstairs.

Tonya said, "Who told you to bring that motherfucking dog in my motherfucking house? The bitch had the nerve to bark at me!" Jamal went downstairs. She said, "Where the hell you get that dog from?"

He said one of Ronald's peoples gave him the dog. He said they were moving to a place where they cannot have any pets. She said, "Did you ask me if you could move this dog here?"

He said, "Come on, Mother. Please can I keep her? Come on, Mama."

Ronald was saying, "Let him keep the dog."

She said, "You shut the fuck up because your ass can leave and the dog can stay. Jamal, this is your responsibility. You are going to take care of the dog, meaning you are going to walk the dog, feed it, and clean that bitch.

He said, "Her name is April."

She said, "I am going to call her bitch of a dog who barked at me," so I burst out laughing again because she was tripping, so after Tonya was done raising hell about that dog, she came upstairs and was talking to Damien about his day in school. He said he had a good day in school. Before she left his room, she told him to start his homework, then she came in the room and said, "Hey, baby! Congratulations again, baby."

I said, "Thank you again, baby" and gave her a hug and a kiss and told her I loved her. She said she loved me too. She said she brought some more of them school lunch boxes home. I heard Jamal calling. Ronald asked what he wanted.

Jamal said, "Who the fuck is you talking to? I am hungry. Go and fix me something to eat."

Ronald said, "What do you want to eat?"

Jamal said, "I don't know."

So Ronald said, "You want some fried chicken?"

Jamal said no.

Ronald said, "You want some chicken fajitas?"

Jamal said, "Yeah, that sounds good," so Ronald went downstairs and made everybody chicken fajitas with the sour cream in the sauce on the side. One thing about Ronald, that man can cook. Everybody was in there grubbing. The food was good. So after me and Tonya were done eating, she took the plate downstairs and washed the dishes. She yelled upstairs to Jamal and told him he needed to walk the dog because it looked like she had to go to the bathroom, so he called Ronald and told him to walk the dog for him. Ronald said, "Look here, motherfucker. I am not your slave," but Ronald ended up walking April.

After Tonya was done washing the dishes, she came back upstairs, and we watched a movie together, so she ended up falling asleep. I continued to watch. When the movie was done, I cut the TV off and went to sleep.

I woke up the next morning around about seven. I washed my face and brushed my teeth. Tonya had woken up and washed her face and brushed her teeth as well, so she asked me what I had to do that day.

"I got to go to Target for orientation, then from there, I am going to work and unload a truck."

She said okay. She said she had to go up social services, so Tonya went downstairs to get a pair of her pants, then all I heard was, "Oh hell no! Jamal!" real loud. I went downstairs to see what was going on. There were piles of shit on the floor as well as piss that was red. I thought something was wrong with the dog because its piss was red, but I later found out that female dogs had periods. She was in heat. It was summer. That piss had a smell that stank like no other. That shit had the whole downstairs jamming. That's how bad it was. Tonya went upstairs and went in Jamal's room and woke him up.

He said, "Come on, Ma. You woke me up for that?"

She said, "You damn right I woke you up. Go downstairs and clean that shit up." Ronald was sleeping in Jamal's room on the floor. Jamal woke up Ronald and told him to go downstairs and clean the piss and the shit up. He said, "I can't believe this shit. A brother can't get any beauty sleep around here. This is some bullshit."

I was leaving the kitchen as Ronald was walking toward it. He said, "Morning, Q."

I said, "Morning," and I went back upstairs. Tonya had woken Damien up for school. I went in me and Tonya's room. She was getting dressed to go up to social service. Now I had got dressed for orientation early because I was going to walk Tonya to the bus stop. When Tonya was ready, I walked her to the bus. Once I made sure she was on the bus, I went back into the house. Damien was leaving the house for school. He only had one more week, then he would be out of school for summer break, so I told Damien to have a good day in school. I went in the house and upstairs to me and Tonya's room to watch a little TV until 8:30, then I left and caught the subway to the 35.

I arrived at Target a half hour early. I'd rather be early than late, so I waited in the lunchroom till 10:00 a.m. I went upstairs to the orientation room. It was me and about six other people. It was two other night shift workers and the three day shift workers, so they went over all the requirements of the day shift workers as well as their pay and safety regulations. Then they went over all the requirements for the night shift workers as well as pay and safety regulations, so before the orientation was over, they let us know that we had to come back the next day and take a safety test on the computer as well as fill out our tax forms on the computer, so after I was done with orientation, I went and caught the bus down to OST.

When I arrived at the warehouse, the truck was there, so I went in the bathroom and changed my clothes. I came out the bathroom and unloaded the truck.

I was done unloading the truck at 2:30 p.m. I went in the bathroom and washed up. I went and caught the 35 bus to the subway and walked home after I got off the subway.

When I got in the house, I went in me and Tonya's room, got my clothes, and went and got in the shower. When I got out, I got dressed and gathered the clothes, went downstairs, and washed our clothes. Now Jamal and Ronald had left out the house, but they did not take the dog with them. They locked the dog in his room. I said to myself that dog was going to piss and shit all over that room. Every time I went upstairs, the dog would bark and scratch at the door, so after I put the clothes in the washing machine, I fixed myself something to eat, and I went upstairs in me and Tonya's room and watched TV. Then I went back downstairs and washed my dishes and got the clothes out the washing machine to hang them up on the line. I went back into the house and mopped the kitchen floor, the dining room floor, and the living room floor. After I was done mopping, I went upstairs in me and Tonya's room and watched TV. I called Pat and told him that I would not be able to work the next day because I had to go back up to Target to fill out some more papers. He said okay. I also gave him the number of the truck that I unloaded that day, so after I was done talking to Pat, I went back downstairs to see if the floor was dry. It was. Then I went outside and got the clothes off the line and brought them into the house. After I was done with that, I went upstairs and played Call of Duty: Modern Warfare survival mode. As I was playing the game, I could hear somebody unlocking the front door. I figured it was probably Damien, and it was, so I continued to play the game. I could hear the microwave warming whatever food Damien put inside, so as I am playing the game, my phone began to ring. I looked and saw it was Tonya, so I answered the phone. I said, "What up, baby?"

She said, "Nothing, just thinking about you."

I said, "I am thinking about you too, baby."

She said she was off the next day, that the day care center would be closed, so I asked her if she was on her way home. She said yeah.

I said okay.

She said, "Is Damien in the house?"

I said, "Yeah, he downstairs."

She said okay, she would see me when she got home. I said, "True that." After I was done talking to Tonya, I unpaused the game. Now I could hear Damien come upstairs.

He said, "What up, Q?"

I said, "What up?"

He said, "You trying to play NBA 2K?"

I said, "Yeah, we can play a couple of games," so I could see that he got even nicer since the last time I played the game, so he won the first game, and I won the two games. After that, we played a couple of games of Modern Warfare. I could hear the front door being unlocked. It was Tonya. I went downstairs. I gave her a kiss and a hug. I saw that the trash needed to be emptied, so I took out the trash. I went back into the house, and as I was shutting the front door, the dog started barking. Tonya was like, "Shut up, bitch." She could not stand the dog ever since the dog barked at her, so I went back upstairs and called my baby mother. I talked to my daughter, and I told her I would come get her Friday. After I was done talking, I told her, "I love you, Kiwi doodle," so her mother got back on the phone. She asked how the interview went.

I said, "I got the job," and she said congratulations. I said thank you.

She said, "When do you start working?"

I said, "Thursday night."

She said, "Damn, that's on your birthday."

I said, "Yeah."

I could hear Tonya coming upstairs. I said to my baby mother, "I'm going to be working both jobs." I noticed the look on Tonya's face. She was upset that I told my baby mother that I was going to be working both jobs, so she said I was going to be tired as hell working both jobs. She said, "When are you going to get any sleep?"

I said, "When I get off work at Target, it will be around 7:00 a.m. to 8:00 a.m. As soon as I leave there, I am going straight to the warehouse I would be working at for that day. I am going to unload two trucks, then after I unload them two trucks, I am going to get some sleep because my shift with Target doesn't start till after Target closes, which is around 10:00 p.m. I got more than enough time to get some sleep."

She said okay. I said I would be there to pick up Kiwi that Friday. She said okay. I told her I would talk to her later, and we hung up the phone.

After I got off the phone, Tonya was saying, "Why you tell your baby mother you are going to work both jobs? Don't be surprised if she takes you down for child support."

I said, "Negative, my baby mother is not a gold digger." I told her me and my baby mother, our daughter would be four next year, and my baby mother had not taken me down for child support once. Why? Because I take care of my responsibilities. I said, "I don't know the dudes you used to talk to that had them type of problems, but this father doesn't have them type of problems. My daughter don't want for nothing. My baby mother doesn't have to call me for anything pertaining my daughter because everything is taken care of— clothes, shoes, food, and this house and her mother's house. My baby mother said out of all her children's father, I am the best father. She is not saying that just to say it. I noticed every time I would defend my baby mother and my daughter, she would get upset. For example I went and brought my daughter three pairs of shoes. She was like, "Why you buy her all them shoes?"

I said, "Don't tell me how to spend my money. You don't say anything when I am buying you $300 to $400 pocketbooks." This shit should have had a brother pack his shit up and leave. You don't have love for my daughter, then you do not have love for me. Tonya was jealous of a three-year-old. You would think she would be proud to have a man who was taking care of his responsibility, but she was not. I should have left, but I didn't because I genuinely loved her unconditionally, and my love for her would cost me; it would be my downfall.

So after me and Tonya were done arguing, I went downstairs and got me something to drink. I already know what type of night it was going to be. We both pissed off. I had no rap for her, and she felt the same way. Still, I went back upstairs into me and Tonya's room. I got in the bed and went to sleep. I woke up the next morning, washed my face, and brushed my teeth, so after I was done, I went back in the room. Tonya was still sleeping, so I got dressed. I woke Damien up for school, then I went downstairs and made breakfast for everyone. After I was done eating, I told Tonya there was breakfast downstairs. I covered the food up, then I walked to the subway. I got on the subway and got off and walked around the corner to the 35 bus. When the bus got there, it was crowded. I got on the bus anyway.

When I got to Target and went upstairs, the lady who worked in the office pulled up the safety quiz. I passed the quiz for the safety regulations. It was very easy, and it was common sense, so after I was done with that, she pulled up the tax forms. I filled them out. Something about that day did not feel right. You know how you get that gut feeling that something is not right? That's how it was, but I could not pinpoint what it was. It was not the issue me and Tonya were having. It was something else, so after I was done filling out the tax forms, the woman who pulled up everything on the computer said I was done, so I left Target and went and caught the bus the 35 to the Subway. The whole time on the ride home, I could feel in my gut that something was not right. Something told me not to go back to the house. I should have gone with my first instinct, but I did not, so I went home. When I got in the house, I fixed me something to eat and went upstairs.

Tonya was lying down watching TV, so I started eating. I looked at the time. It was like 12:50 p.m., so after I was done eating, I took the plate downstairs and washed it out, went back upstairs. Tonya had gone back to sleep, so I lay down next to her.

About ten to fifteen minutes later, I hear a big boom. I jumped straight up like, "What the fuck was that?" I heard another big boom. I went in the hall at the top of the stairs. It was the police was knocking down the door. Tonya had woken up by the second boom. She was like, "What the hell was that?" so I was at the top of the stairs now. The door was fucked up, but it was not opened to where they could get in the house.

I said, "These bitches. Man, I fucking hate the police," so these bitches hit the door for a third time, and when they hit the door this time, the door shattered in two. The whole door was in the floor. I was looking at these bitches shaking my head. When the door was knocked down, they ran in the house with their guns out, saying, "Baltimore city police, put your hands up and walk downstairs with your hands up."

They said, "Is anyone else in the house?"

Then he saw Tonya right behind me. He said, "Miss, put your hands up," so she did, so they put the handcuffs on us and got us two chairs out the kitchen. We sat down in the chairs. A black dude who was the sergeant was dumping all the bags with the pocketbooks out on the floor. A white police officer came through the front door and said, "So this is the Piru family? This is a Blood family. Where are the guns and the drugs? Who is a Keith Noble?"

So Tonya was like that's her son, so he said, "You are the mother of a high-ranked Blood member.

She said, "I don't know what you are talking about."

He said, "Save us the trouble. Tell us where the drugs and the guns at so we don't have to tear down this house."

Me and Tonya said it at the same time, "We don't know what you are talking about."

He said, "Have it your way," so about three of them went upstairs. The sergeant officer was asking Tonya, "How are you able to afford all these designer pocketbooks? You live in the projects."

She said, "Just because I live in the project doesn't mean I cannot afford the designer pocket books."

He said, "These got to be fake pocketbooks."

She said not one of her pocketbooks is fake.

This dude sounded like a hater because he could not afford to buy his bitch a designer pocketbook. This dude was looking through all the pocketbooks hoping to find something so they could lock us up, so me and Tonya could hear them tearing the rooms upstairs, destroying them. They got to Jamal's room, and the door was locked, so the white police officer came downstairs and asked Tonya, "Who sleeps in the room right there at the top of the stairs?"

She said her son Jamal. He said, "Do you got a key to unlock the door?" She said no, so he said, "We are going to have to break the door down," so he asked if there was a little dog in the room because he could hear the dog barking.

She said, "It is a shih tzu."

He said okay, so they ended up breaking the door down. We could hear them tearing the door apart, so after they were done searching upstairs, they came downstairs. The black sergeant was still searching in the kitchen, so they called me in the kitchen and asked me if I knew Keith.

I said, "No, I don't know him."

They asked if I lived there.

I said, "No, I am just visiting. I don't know anything about nothing," so they told me to go sit back in the living room. They called Tonya and started asking her questions about Keith. She said she didn't know anything, so she asked if she could call her son, which is Keith. They said no. They already raided his house first. These bitches did not find anything but a roach, white boy, and an ashtray in some clear bags that did not contain any drugs in them. Them bitches was mad. They did not find anything, so one of the officers asked the sergeant if they were locking me and Tonya up. He asked them what they found upstairs. He said some blue bags that did not contain any drugs as well as a roach, white boy joints, which means, for those who don't know, top paper. He said a roach that smelled like it has marijuana in it. So the black sergeant said, "No, we are not going to lock them, then he said, "Matter of fact, call the lieutenant and see what he says," so he called the lieutenant in.

He said, "Yeah, lock them up."

These bitches must not meet their quota of arrests that week because they were taking us to jail for that bullshit. These pigs were bitches. They were just mad they did not find anything that was worth raiding. Them bitches were so mad. You should have seen their faces from the beginning of the house raid to the end. In the beginning, them bitches just knew they were going to find drugs, guns, and a lot of money. Then the bitches were upset, so they allowed me and Tonya to put some shoes on our feet, so we put our shoes on. They walked me and Tonya outside to the paddy wagon, which means the police van. They put Tonya on one side of the van and put me on the other side. As they were bringing me out the house, I noticed my baby mother's best friend was outside on the phone. I could hear her talking to my baby mother. She said, "Girl, the police just raided your baby father's house. They are locking him up."

I noticed they had a police car out there, and I could see that Keith was in the back of the police car. They drove off with our front door wide open. I already knew where we were going—to Central Booking. Tonya did too, even though this was her first time being locked up. She'd heard stories about Central Booking from me and her son. I told Tonya, "We are about to get our own recognizance."

She said, "What does that mean?"

I said, "That means you don't have to pay for a bail. Something that is time-consuming when we get down here at Central Booking is waiting to see the commissioner. Depending on how crowded it is when we get down Central Booking, we may not see the commissioner until the next day. It could be in the morning or in the afternoon."

She said, "Don't you start work tomorrow night?"

I said, "Yeah, we should be out before it's time for me to go to work. Also people who get their own recognizance, we call them walk-through, meaning all they are waiting to do is see the commissioner, and they have gone back on the street. Usually you see people getting their own recognizance when the charges are minor as well as if it is a person's first time getting locked up and the charges are minor. They will let them out on their own recognizance. The charges that they are about to charge us with are petty and minor."

She said, "Where they put you at while you waiting to see the commissioner?"

I said, "They are going to put us in the bullpen. When we get down here at Central Booking, they are going to separate us. You going on the side of Central Booking with the women, and they are going to put me on the side with the brothers. Get ready to hear a lot of women talk about their cases or tell their stories."

I told Tonya she would be entertained until she saw the commissioner because when you're in the bullpen with twenty to thirty other people, somebody, if not half of the bull pen, will be talking about how they got locked up or how much money they were getting on their block. You are going to hear stories. I have done heard so many stories from being locked up in the past. I heard stories from brothers saying, "I was getting so much money, at home was getting bricks, I was running this block," and when you see that same person uptown, they be on the corner asking for change, or they be out there getting high. Everybody wants to be somebody important, so dudes be making up stories.

I noticed as me and Tonya were in the police paddy wagon, the officer was driving crazy. He was hitting every bump in the street. That's how crazy he was driving, so I yelled, "You still have two people in the back of here, and we do not have any seat belts on." I am not going to lie, every street in the city of Baltimore is fucked up. Now when you go toward the county, the streets are way better. In the city, you always see government workers fixing the street, but they never get no better. I think they be milking the city on the clock because they be fixing the street for months, and when they get done, the street are worse than before they started working on them. When you drive through my city, all you see is these city workers working on the ground or clean up trash in the alleys.

So me and Tonya was almost at Central Booking. When we got to the jail, they drove through the gate and drove up to the door. They took me out the paddy wagon and stood next to the door. I could see through the door. There was nobody but like four people waiting to see the nurse, so the police got Tonya out the back of the paddy wagon and walked her up to the door that was farther up. That was the women's entrance to the jail, so they took Tonya inside the jail.

They opened the door, and I walked in the jail, then I walked through the metal detector then sat down. I waited to see the nurse. I had three people in front of me. I was expecting it to be more crowded than it was, but I was glad it was not crowded because that means there was a chance that we could see the commissioner faster or earlier. I also noticed that Keith, Tonya's son, did not get brought down here. When we got to here, they had that dude in the back of the police car. I guess when they raided his house, they did not find anything to arrest him, so they just held him in the police car so he would not call his mother and give her the heads-up and let her know that they would be coming to her house next. Them pigs just knew they were going to find something. So after they raided me and Tonya's house, they must have let Keith go because if not, he would be down Central Booking. I was next to see the nurse. They started bringing more people in the jail, so the nurse called me to sit in the chair and took my blood pressure and my temperature. Then she asked me a bunch of medical questions, so after I answered, I went across from where nurse was at and sat down the next step.

One of the most degrading things as a man when you get locked up is the strip search. They do these strip searches to make sure no one is bringing in contraband, which is drugs, or to make sure nobody is bringing in no sort of weapons. The methods they have you do will have you feeling and looking less than a human. First, they have you take off your shoes and socks and hand your shoes to the officer. That officer will check your shoes and socks, then they tell you to remove your shirt, and you got to give them your shirt. They will shake your shirt out, then they tell you to remove your pants. Then you got to give the pants to the officer, and they will check your pockets to make sure no drugs or weapons are inside. They will also shake the pants out. Then they will tell you to remove your underwear. This shit is degrading, but that's not it. Then they tell you to lift your balls up and squat and cough from the front. Then they tell you to turn around and squat and cough with your back turn toward them. This shit is the most degrading thing as a man, and the whole time it's a man who is doing the check. The woman has to go through the same procedure, but they have a woman who does their check. Now the reason they do the squat and cough is because people be smuggling drugs and weapons in their ass. That shit is the most embarrassing and degrading thing as a human being.

Now I had one more person in front of me for the strip search. They had started bringing a good amount of people in the jail. The person who was in front of me had gone in the room to be searched. I was up next. After the dude left the room, the CO called me in. This shit was degrading, so after I went through the search, the CO walked me over there to the window where this woman asked me if I had any property, money, jewelry, ID, or license. Now the CO handcuffed me to the ledge that was connected to the window.

The lady at the window asked me what my address was. I gave her my 420 East Biddle Street address. She asked me my weight and height. I said I weighed 190, and my height was about 5'6". She asked if I had any jewelry or anything that was going into property. I said no, so she said I was done, and she put a band around my wrist. The band can be scanned so that the CO knows which inmate it was, so after she put the band around my arm, she signaled for the CO to take the handcuff off and walked me down to the fingerprint room. When I got in the room, there were about five people waiting to get their fingerprints taken. I sat down and waited until it was my turn. So after she was done with the first person she was fingerprinting, he went outside the room. Now the phone was outside the fingerprint room. There were like four phones lined up on the wall spaced out from each other, and across the phones are the bullpens. After you get your fingerprints taken, then the CO tells you to go make your free phone call. After you make your free phone call, then the CO scans the band that's on your wrist. It allows the CO to know what bullpen you are in because they also scan the side of the door, so the CO scans the side of the door, then she scans the wrist of the inmate, then the inmate goes in the bullpen. Once you're in the bullpen, what you are waiting for is to see the commissioner to see if you are going to get a bail or if you are going to have to wait until you go to court. I had one more person in front of me before I got my fingerprints taken. After the CO was done taking his fingerprints, she took my fingerprints. I went and used the phone. I called my mother. She answered the phone like, "Oh my god, what are you locked up for?"

I said, "For something petty."

She asked if I got a bail.

I said I hadn't seen the commissioner yet.

She said, "Don't you start your new job tomorrow?"

I said, "Yeah. We should be released before I go to work tomorrow."

She said, "We?"

"Me and Tonya," she said. "They locked Tonya up too. Them pigs are petty."

The CO said, "Five more minutes," so I told my mother I loved her, and I would talk to her when I got home. When I hung up the phone, the CO came and opened up the bullpen, so she scanned the door of the bullpen and then she scanned my wrist and then I went in to the bullpen. Now all that was in the bullpen was one toilet that was connected to the sink. It also had a cement bench on both sides of the bullpen. It had a window so the CO could monitor the bullpen. Now they sometimes put twenty-five to thirty people in the bullpen, and there's nowhere to sit and sleep on the floor. It's like when people put their animal in the cage after that animal did something bad. When a person gets locked up, it's like their life is equal to an animal's life. Here's why I say that. Because when we get locked up, we are put in a cage. We are fed food that I would not feed to my animal. You have to be told when to eat, when to sleep. You are stripped of all your human rights. Prison is degrading for any human being. Jail is legalized slavery here. Why I say that is because the government pays each jail as well as prison institutions $33,274 a person. Now the prison system makes billions of dollars; it is a billion-dollar business that will continue to make money, and it is sad to say because it is legalized slavery. As long as people continue to commit crimes and continue breaking the law, the correctional system is always going to make money off inmates. Even when an inmate gets his or her time, they have the option to work or go to school, or they can get into a program. Now I hear people complaining about them making less than minimum wage when brother and sister who are incarcerated makes 86 to 93 cents a day, which is slavery.

I know what people may say—"I would not work that job." Now I say a lot of people who are locked up are not fortunate to have family members who send them money orders every week or once a month, so that's why people get a job as well as those who can earn good conduct credit, which is taking time off your release date. Now you have two release dates. Inmates who can earn good conduct credits, those inmates have a maximum release date and a minimum release date. Your maximum release date is you doing all your time to the door, and this usually means that inmate must have kept catching tickets, breaking rules in categories such as fighting tickets, getting caught with contraband, which is drugs and weapons or cell phones. Now these are just a few tickets that you can catch because they are illegal and prohibited for an inmate to have. Now if an inmate catches a ticket for any of these categories, they would have to go in front of a disciplinary hearing officer. The hearing can go several ways. If you got found guilty or pled guilty, you could get locked up, which is called disciplinary segregation, which means you will be taken to lockup for every amount of days or months you got found guilty of or pled guilty of. Sometimes when a person keeps catching tickets, they can get put on lockup for years. Now that is one of the ways. Another way is you can get some or all your good time or good days taken away from you, meaning if you are able to earn good days and you have a chance to be released early on your minimum release and you catch a ticket and the hearing officer decides to take all your good days, then you get released on your maximum release date. For example, if my minimum release is 2020 and my maximum release date is 2021 and I catch a ticket and the disciplinary officer says, "I am going to take all your good days," that means I am maxing out. I am doing all my time to the door, which means all the good conduct credit that I have earned that would have gotten me home early in 2020 is gone. I could have worked a job and earned them credit or I could have gone to school and earned the credit; however, a person earns the credit, but when you catch a ticket, some of the credit or all the good conduct credit can be taken away now. There are other ways you can lose good conduct credit and also get lockup time.

Another way is to beat the ticket by getting found not guilty. You can also get cell restrictions, meaning for whatever time the disciplinary officer says. It could be thirty days or a week in cell restrictions, meaning you stay in your cell all day and can only come out your cell for chow, which is breakfast, lunch, or dinner. The only time you can exit the cell is when you are taking a shower.

Now no recreation means no dayroom. The dayroom is where everyone goes to watch TV if you don't have a TV, and your cell or inmates go to the dayroom to use the phone to call your people uptown.

Now in the bullpen that I was in, there were about fifteen to twenty people, and one of them was a dope fiend. He was going through withdrawal because he had not had any drugs, and most fiends would agree with me when I say this—being locked up and having to go through withdrawal is like death, especially if that drug addict has a bad habit. The reason I say it's like death to that drug addict is because by not being able to get their drugs, they begin to start throwing up, they have diarrhea, their nose starts to run, they start to get the chills and hot and cold sweats, and they can't eat because if they do, they are going throw it back up or shit it back out. I say for the first five to six days, it is rough for a drug addict.

One time when I was locked up, I had drug addict as my cell buddy. He was going through withdrawals. This man moved his mattress right next to the bullet, which means right next to the toilet. He stayed in the cell all day. He did not eat. All he did was sleep in the bullpen.

There was a brother in there who was going through it. He had just gotten released from prison after serving ten years. He said his homeboys came and picked him up from the institution he was at. He said he did not go straight home. They drove around. He said they ended up stopping at a store, and when they left the store and got back into the car, the driver pulled out the parking lot and got a block away from the store. They got pulled over by the police. They were smoking weed, and the car smelled of weed. He thought that it was just weed, so the police officers ended up taking each person out the car. The person who telling what happened, he was sitting in the passenger seat. Now when the police ended up searching the car, they found a gun on the passenger side, so the police asked everybody in the car whose gun it was. Nobody said the gun was theirs, so the police locked up everyone who was in that car up and brought them to Central Booking. He said he did not even get the chance to see his daughter since she was born. He was in there shedding tears. Everybody in that bullpen said that shit was fucked up. A lot of people in the bullpen were telling him it was going to work in his favor. He still had his release papers stating he just got released from prison. He had that old head, which means older person, to look at his charge papers. He must have thought about that shit because while the old head was reading, he went over there and snatched his papers back from the old head's hands. He said, "You all don't understand. I just left prison to be rebooked on some shit. I had no knowledge that a gun was in the car."

Brothers in the bullpen was like, "People are fucked up. Knowing that you was leaving the institution you was at, going to come pick you up knowing that they were riding dirty," which means with an illegal firearm or illegal drugs, but for the dude's people not to let him know before he got in the car that they were riding dirty, that's what makes them dudes fucked up; they disregarded the fact that this man just walked out them prison gates. They did not give him the option to say no. I know if that was me and I just did all that time and my homeboys came pick me up and let me know they were riding dirty, I am going to be like, "No, I am good. Let me use your phone so I can call somebody else to come pick me up." I am not taking no chances, but you got cruddy people who won't let you know before you get in that there's a gun or drugs in their car.

Now it has been hours since me and Tonya had gotten locked up. I could tell that we were going to see the commissioner tomorrow. It looked like we were staying the night in jail, which was crazy. They had brought bag lunches for dinner. Shift change had happened, which meant the COs that worked in the morning went home, and the COs who worked the night shift had come to work. Shift change time was usually at 5:00 p.m. or at 6:00 p.m.

Now the bag lunches had sweaty meat, which is bologna that be sweating, as well as cheese that doesn't ever melt. I don't know what the fuck kind of cheese that is, but the cheese looks like rubber, and it shines. It looks like play cheese, something that's not real as well as something that a person should not be eating. Also, the bag lunches had cookies, which was the best thing in the bag as well as Goldfish.

Now our drinks was base in a plastic bag that you had to bite through to drink. For those of you who have never been to jail and don't know what base is, people can use base to dye their hair as well as to wash clothes. Base used to be clear with sugar in it. Now what they started doing is adding food coloring in the base, and it changes from looking clear like bleach to looking like red juice or blue juice or whatever food coloring they put into the base. Even if they change the color, none of that shit matters 'cause that shit still is base. A lot of people drink the base including myself. They say you should not drink the base because it fucks with your sperm, but when they make the base right, adding enough sugar, and it's cold, that shit is good. If they don't add enough sugar, that shit is not good.

Now there's also mustard packs or mayonnaise or ketchup packs. People would trade a bag lunch for a pack of cookies. They would take their cookies out the bag and leave the sweaty meat and the Goldfish. A lot of people would take the trade. I don't see why they did the trade. The cookies are the best thing in the bag. The rest of that shit is garbage. Now the drug addict, he was not eating anything; he was just holding the bag lunch.

Now the bullpen was crowded. You had people lying on the floor people sitting on the cement bench I was sitting on the floor. They called me and Tonya at the same time the next day, around about 1:00 or 12:00 p.m. When the CO came to get me, she did not know what bullpen I was in, so she called my name out, so I yelled back, "Yeah?"

She said, "You Quentin?"

I said yes.

She said, "Come on, you got to go see the commissioner." She told me to walk down the hallway and stand on the right-hand side of the wall while she locked the bullpen door back. You would have thought the commissioner's room was upstairs somewhere the way she said, "Stand on the right-hand side of the wall." The commissioner's room was just around the corner. Now after she locked the bullpen door, she walked down the hallway and escorted me around the corner. When we got around the corner, I could see Tonya in the hallway. Tonya went in the commissioner's room. The room she went in was one room up from the room I went in. I saw her, and she saw me, and we both started smiling at each other. The CO unlocked the door to the commissioner's room. I walked in the room.

It was a woman commissioner. She asked me if I still stayed on Biddle Street. She asked if the number they had on file in the computer was the same. The reason they asked if the address is the same is because if you bail out or get your own recognizance, or even if you don't get a bail, they send a letter to your address that's on file or on the computer, letting you know when your court date is. Also, they will send you a letter letting you know what office you can go to get a public defender for your court date, so she ended up giving me my own recognizance, and she told me what day I had to go to court, which was thirty days from that day, so she printed out the papers to my court date as well as papers to give to the CO stating I got my own recognizance.

After I was done, I gave the release papers to the CO. I went in the hallway, and Tonya was in the hallway. She said she got her own recognizance as well, so the COs walked us down the hallway to the bullpens to be processed to be released. They put Tonya in the bullpen right next to mine. She was in the bullpen by herself. I had three people in front of me waiting to be processed for their release. Now they ended up processing Tonya first, so after Tonya got processed, they hit the button and buzzed her out. She walked to the lobby and then she walked out the front door. She was outside the jail.

After the CO processed the people in front of me, she called me to be processed. When she was done, she hit the buzzer to open the door. I left and went through the front. There was Tonya waiting outside, so I gave her a hug and a kiss. She said, "You called it with us getting our own recognizance. Don't you start work tonight with Target?"

I said, "Yeah, I do."

She said, "We got out just in time."

I said, "Yeah, that was a blessing," so we began to walk to my grandmother's house. I knocked on the door, and she said, "Who is it?"

I said, "Your grandson."

She said, "You all must be just getting released."

I said, "Yeah, I wanted to come and check on you."

She said she wanted me to go to the corner store and play her numbers and get her some scratch-offs. I did, so her and Tonya sat down there and talked. When I came back from the store, I gave her the numbers and the scratch-offs and gave her a hug and a kiss on the cheek. I told her I loved her.

She said, "Don't you start work at Target tonight?"

I said, "Yeah, that's why I am trying to get in the house and get a little bit of sleep before I go to work."

My grandmother said, "Thank you for coming to check up on as well as going to the store for me."

I said, "That's no problem, Ma. That's what I am here for. Let me know if you need anything else."

Tonya said, "See you later, Grandma."

"See you later as well."

Me and Tonya left and started walking home. When we arrived home, we noticed that the front door was boarded up because there was no front door. Anybody who didn't know somebody was living in there would have thought the house was abandoned, which means a vacant house. We had to go around to the back door to knock. Jamal came and opened the back door. He said, "What the hell happened?" so Tonya was like, "That motherfucking Keith. They raided his house and then they raided our house. They found a white boy roach that they said contained weed," and she said, "They found the weed in your room."

He said that was not weed. He said, "I had rolled up some tobacco in some top paper," so Tonya said, "They said it was weed." She said also they found small plastic bags that did not contain any drugs.

He said, "That shit crazy. They just wanted to lock you and Q up. Me and Ronald and Damien straightened up the house. He said he came home, and the front door was wide open. He saw all his mother's pocketbooks thrown everywhere. He said he went upstairs and saw that in every room, shit was thrown everywhere. He said the maintenance man came and put a board up at the front door and told him that somebody would have to call the rental office and put in the claim for the front door to be replaced with a new door as well as the room door upstairs. He said Keith came down the house that night and asked if they had heard from us. Jamal told him no. Jamal had asked Keith what happened, so Keith said, "Remember the old car I had? The black car?"

He said, "Yeah, I remember the car."

He said, "I was not using it no more, but I still have tags on the car. When I fix my new car, I would park over there by my old car, and I would place a gun on the tire of the old car. I would leave the gun under the car tire. I don't know what happened. All I know is they raided my house, talking, 'Is this your license plate to your car?'"

He'd said, "Yeah, that's my old car. That car been sitting there for a while. I was about to get it fix and sell it."

The officer showed him a picture of a gun and told him, "Does this gun look familiar?"

He said no, so one of the officers said he was lying. He said, "Well, why is the gun found on the tire of a car registered in your name?"

He said, "I don't know. That car has been sitting on that block for months. Anybody could have put that gun right there. I do live in the projects."

They started searching his apartment. He said he asked if he could call his mother. The officer said, "Who? Tonya Jackson? We are about to raid her house next." They did not find anything in his house, so he said they brought him downstairs out of his apartment and then put him in the police car so he would not call his mother and let her know that they were about to raid her house; he could not give her the heads-up, so he said asked why they were searching his mother's house the whole time he was in the police car. He said after they were done, he saw the police bring me and his mother out the house in handcuffs and put us in the paddy wagon. He said when the paddy wagon pulled off, they took him out the police car and took the handcuffs off him and gave him the police report. He said somebody reported the gun on the tire. He said to Jamal that one of the people who he sold crack to in his apartment building came and knocked on his door and told him that they were towing his car, so he went downstairs to see what was going on. He said he saw them towing the car, and the police was over there. He said he did not walk over, and he did not go back in the apartment building. He said he walked around the corner. Somebody from their house called the police, informed them that the person they were looking for just went around the corner, so they got into their car and drove around the corner, and they grabbed Keith and told him they were just about to come to his apartment. They got the keys out his pocket and went and searched his apartment and did not find anything.

Tonya ended up calling the rental office to file a claim so they could come and fix the front door. I had forgotten that it was my birthday. I turned twenty-four that day. I only realized it was my birthday when my mother called me to see if I made it home. When I answered the phone, she said, "Happy birthday, my son."

I said, "Is today the sixth?" She said yes.

I said, "Thank you, I appreciate it. I love you."

She said, "I need a couple of dollars."

I said, "How much you need?"

She said, "About $50 dollars." She said she had somebody with a truck that was going to move the rest of her stuff from my grandmother's house to Sharon's house.

I said, "Okay, when're you coming to get it?"

She said she was making her way over here now. I said okay. I said, "Grandma is calling my phone now." I told my mother I would see her when she got there and clicked over and started talking to my grandmother. She said, "Why you didn't remind me that today was your birthday?"

I said, "Ma, I forgot myself, Ma."

She said, "I just wanted to wish you a happy birthday, and what do you want for your birthday?"

I said, "Nothing."

She said, "I am going to get you something anyway."

I said, "Okay, I love you, Ma. Thank you."

She said, "Happy birthday again, and I wish you many more."

I said, "Thank you again, Ma. It's just another day, Ma."

She said, "It's just another year that God has blessed you to see."

I said, "You right, Ma, because so many people in our city are not making it to see age 19 or 20, let alone 24. For some people I am blessed that I have made it to see 24."

She said, "That is so true."

I said, "I love you, Ma, and I will talk to you later."

She said, "I love you too," so after I got off the phone with my grandmother, I could hear a knock at the door and could hear Tonya opening the door. I could hear my mother's voice, so I got the money and went downstairs. My mother said, "What's up, my oldest son?"

I gave my mother a hug and a kiss on her cheek and then I gave her the money. She said she had to go. She had Cornell and the person driving the truck out there waiting. I gave my mother another hug and kiss and told her I loved her again. She said she loved me more and left. I walked outside. I could see Cornell waving. I said, "What up?"

When they pulled off, I went back into the house. Tonya was still downstairs in the kitchen, and she told me that the maintenance people would be there on Friday to put a new front door on.

I said, "That was fast usually. They drag their feet with repairing things." I gave Tonya a hug and kiss and told her I loved her and I was going to get in the shower and get a little sleep before I got to work that night.

She said, "Okay, baby, I love you too," so I went in got in the shower. After I got out the shower, I got dressed, brushed my teeth, went in me and Tonya's room, and went to sleep.

I woke up around about 8:00 p.m. I washed my face and brushed my teeth. I got dressed and put my Target shirt on and some khaki pants. I gave Tonya a hug and a kiss and left the house at 8:30 p.m. I walked to the subway and caught the subway to the 35. When I got to work, it was about 9:30 p.m. When I got there, the store had a half an hour before they closed, so I just went in the break room. I could hear one of the employees on the loudspeaker letting the customers know that the store would be closing in five minutes, and to please make their way to the checkout line, so after the store closed, my shift began. I punched in. They had me on the schedule for getting off 2:00 a.m. so supervisor said I could stay to 7:00 or 8:00 a.m.

I said, "I am just going to clock out to go home after I work my hours," so he said okay. The first day they did not start me work on the truck. They had me sorting the items that came down the assembly line from who was unloading the truck. You had to sort your household items from your food. You had to make sure everything was sorted right because after the truck would be unloaded and everything what be sorted, we would have to push the items in the aisles according to what was on the pallet and then after every pallet had been put in the aisles, everyone would start picking an aisle and start putting everything where it belonged.

After I worked to 2:00 a.m., I clocked out and went and found the supervisor. He unlocked the front door and let me out the store and locked the door back. I went across the street and waited on the bus. When the bus came down the street, I got on the bus, and it took me to the subway. I got on the subway and got off at the state center across from the unemployment building. After I got off the subway, I walked home.

When I got home, Tonya was up watching TV. She said, "Hey, baby, you home early."

I said, "Yeah, they had my first day time as 10:00 p.m. to 2:00 a.m."

She asked how my first day was. I said okay. She said she got a phone call around about 2:00 a.m. from Bryant's girl saying Bryant beat her up and stole her car. He left her somewhere over East Baltimore.

"That shit crazy. Bryant don't make no sense."

Things would get even crazier the next months, starting on the month of August. Now both Keith and Chantelle's daughter birthday are in the same month, so Tonya and Chantelle came up with the idea that since Keith and Mama shared a birthday in the same month, why not throw them a birthday in the same month—have Mama's birthday during the day and Keith's birthday during the night. It was now two days before Keith and Mama's birthday. I told Keith for his birthday. I was going to buy all the drinks for his birthday party, so Keith picked me and Tonya up and drove us to the liquor store. When we got there, I told him get all the liquor he wanted.

He said, "For real?"

I said yeah, now Keith really was not a drinker, so he was asking the liquor store cashier for a drink called Pinnacle. Tonya said she wanted a bottle of E&J.

I said, "I don't know what type liquor you all ordering. We are in a wholesale liquor store." I told the liquor store cashier to put the big bottle of Hennessy up there. "Put a big bottle of Remy Martin and put a big bottle of Grey Goose." I also said, "Put a big bottle of CIROC and another big bottle of Hennessy up there. Then give me a big bottle of Amsterdam, a big bottle of Patron tequila, and another big bottle of CIROC and Grey Goose."

After we got all the liquor, I paid for everything. The store gave us a big box to put all the liquor in. We left and got in the car with all the liquor and went home. Now when we got in the house, Keith took the box of liquor into the kitchen and took the liquor out of the box and placed the liquor on the counter and started taking pictures of all the liquor, so Jamal came downstairs and was like, "Damn, who all this liquor for?"

Tonya said, "Q brought all this liquor for Keith's birthday party."

Keith said, "Q's a real brother."

Jamal said, "Damn, I can't wait to my birthday party," so Jamal said, "Open a bottle now."

Keith was like, "No, this for my birthday."

Jamal was like, "All this liquor? You are not going to miss one bottle."

Keith said, "Okay, we are going open a bottle. Q, since you brought all the liquor, which one should we open up?

I said, "Open up the Hennessy. We are celebrating your birthday two days before the party."

He said, "Already? Bet," so he opened the Hennessy up. We all got a cup, and everybody pulled their own trouble. That's an old saying. So that man Keith was done and drunk after one cup. Jamal said to Keith, "Boy, you not no drinker. You tap out."

"Kieth kept saying, "My hands are numb. I can't feel my hands."

Tonya said, "Boy, be quiet."

He is like, "Ma, I cannot feel my hand. What's in that liquor?"

Jamal said, "You had a little bit of Hennessy in a cup. That was not even enough Hennessy to even be drunk."

That dude Keith just kept saying, "I can't feel my hand."

I said, "This guy tripping," so after I had drunk my first cup. I went and got another cup. I did not have to work that night, so I got another cup of the Hennessy. I looked at Tonya. She was feeling good, I could tell. That dude Keith left and went picked up Shamika, so Jamal asked Keith if he was driving over East Baltimore. He said yeah. He asked him would he drop him off over Glen's house? Keith said yeah, he would, so they left the house.

Now Damien was over Delicia's house, which is Tonya's sister's house, but she's not her biological sister. Me and Tonya were the only ones home, so I started kissing her on her lips and started kissing and biting her on her neck. Me and Tonya started making love, and that Hennessy had both of us in there sweating while we were making love. After we got done making love, we got into the shower and washed up. Me and Tonya went downstairs and fixed something to eat. After we were done eating, we went upstairs and watched TV and then Tonya went to sleep. I was still watching, then I cut the TV off and went to sleep as well. I woke up to Tonya making breakfast in bed.

I said, "Thank you, baby. I love you, baby. Today I am going to get Mama two pairs of shoes for her birthday tomorrow," so after I was done eating breakfast, I went into the bathroom and washed my face and brushed my teeth, then I got dressed. I asked Tonya if she wanted to go. She said no, she was just going to relax, so I said, "Okay, I love you. I will see you when I get back." I left out the house and caught the 21 bus to the light rail. I got off the light rail at Lexington Market and went into Downtown Locker Room. I got her a pair of the new Jordans and a pair of the new Air Max shoes. After I got the shoes, I paid for them and went and got back on the light rail. I got off the light rail and caught the 21 back up the street to the house. I got off the bus and went in the house and went upstairs, and Tonya was on the phone talking to Chantelle about Mama's party the next day my So she saw the shoe bag, so she was like, "Let me see the shoes." She told Chantelle, "He went and got her some Jordans and a pair of Air Max. They are nice." She liked both of them

Chantelle said thank you. She said she may not fit the Jordans because Mama had something called idiopathic toe walking, which has historically been called habitual toe walking. Mama would not walk on the heels of her feet; she would walk on the tip of her toes, so she could not wear certain shoes. If the shoes could not bend, then Mama would not be able to wear them.

I said, "She probably can fit the Air Max that I brought her."

She said, "Okay, thank you."

"But try both shoes and see which ones fit."

She said, "Okay, thank you again." Now I went downstairs and got myself something to drink. Now I had to work that night, so after I got me something to drink, I went upstairs and got some sleep. When I woke up, it was around about 7:00 p.m. So I got up, washed my face, brushed my teeth, went downstairs, and fixed something to eat. I washed the dishes, and I went upstairs and got dressed.

Tonya said, "Baby, you know it's just 7:30 p.m."

I said, "Yeah, I know. I am just getting ready early."

She asked me if I was off for the party tomorrow. I said yeah. She asked me if my baby mother was bringing Kiwi to Mama's party.

I said, "Yeah, she is bringing Kiwi. I am going to cook for both parties." Tonya and Chantelle were going to get the food for the party, the cake, the piñata, and the candy the next day. She said they were going to have Mama's party around about 1:00 p.m. or 2:00 p.m., and Keith's birthday was going to be around 7:00 p.m. or 8:00 p.m.

I said, "Okay, that sounds like a winner."

She said she invited a couple of her homegirls to the party. She said her niece Jessie was going to be at the party. I said okay. After me and Tonya were done talking, I noticed that it was 8:30 p.m., so I gave Tonya a hug and a kiss and told her I loved her and I would see her tomorrow, so I left the house and locked the front door. I walked to the subway. After I got off the subway, I walked around the corner and waited on the 35 bus. When the bus got there, it was about 9:20 p.m. I saw a couple of people that I worked with on the job at Target when I got on the bus.

When I got to work, I went in the back of the store and checked out my schedule. I was off work the next day. It had my time to clock out at 7:00 a.m. After I saw my schedule, I went in the break room until the store closed.

So after the store closed, I clocked in to start work. I went to the back of the store to the warehouse. They had me unloading the truck, me and another person who worked there, so we started unloading the truck, sending the items down the assembly line, and the other coworkers sorted the items according to what aisles they went to, so after we were done unloading the truck, everybody chose an aisle and started stocking the shelves until around about 1:00 a.m., then one of the night supervisors spoke on the loudspeaker telling everybody to take their fifteen-minute break, so I went and sat down and called Tonya and made sure everybody was okay.

When she answered the phone, I could tell that she was asleep.

I said, "Baby, I just wanted to say I love you and to check up on you and make sure you are good."

She said she was okay and that she loved me too.

I said, "Okay, see you in the morning."

She said okay, so after I got off the phone with Tonya, I went back to work. Around 3:00 a.m., one of the supervisors got on the loudspeaker. "Everybody, take your half-an-hour break, and if anyone wants to buy any food or drink, meet me at register 1," so I went, sat down until 3:30 a.m., then I went back to work now. After my shift was over, I went and clocked out and went and caught the bus. When I got home, it was around about 8:30 a.m. or 9:00 a.m. Tonya was up watching her morning TV shows such as *The Jeffersons* and *Good Times*, so I went in the room and said, "Good morning, baby," gave her a hug and a kiss.

She said, "Good morning, baby. How was your night?"

I said, "It was okay. I am about get in the shower and try to get a couple of hours sleep before Mama's birthday party as well as Keith's birthday party," so I went and got the shower. When I got out, I got dressed and brushed my teeth. When I went in me and Tonya's room, she said, "Baby, Chantelle is about to come pick me up so we can go to the store and pick up some more things for Mama's birthday party."

I said, "Okay, if you are still at the store around twelve in the afternoon, can you call my phone and wake me up so I can get ready?"

She said, "Okay, I will," so I went to sleep, but I could hear when Tonya left the house. I had just gone to sleep, only to be woken up by my phone ringing. It was my mother checking up on me/

I said, "What's going on?"

She said, "Same shit, just a different day." She asked if I had work tonight.

I said, "No, I am off tonight. I actually just not too long ago got off work."

She said okay and asked me if she woke me up.

I said yeah, but she was good. I told her Mama's and Keith's birthday parties are later on today.

She said, "Where is Tonya at?"

I said, "Chantelle came and picked her up to go and get some more things for Mama's birthday party."

She said, "Okay, how is my granddaughter doing?"

I said, "She is good. She will be at the party. Her mother is bringing her over here. What's up with Cornell?"

She said, "He is good. If he could just stop that drinking."

After I was done talking to my mother, I told her I loved her and would talk to her later, so I tried to doze back off to sleep when my phone started to ring again. It was my grandmother, so I answered the phone.

I said, "Good morning, Ma. Are you good?"

She said, "Good morning." She asked if I was just getting off work.

I said, "Yeah, not too long ago I got off work."

She asked me if I had to work that night.

I said, no, I was off.

She said, "I did not want anything but to check up on you and make sure you was okay."

I said, "I am good. How are you doing?"

She said she was doing okay.

I said, "Okay. Is my little brother there?"

She said he had just left the house.

I said, "Okay. When he gets back in the house, tell him to call my phone."

She said, "Okay, I will, because you need to talk to him. He needs to get a job because there's more to life than just running the streets with his friends or going up to the dome and playing basketball. He really needs to find a job."

My grandmother really did not like my little bro. For whatever reason, she said he reminded her of herself when she was younger.

I say she doesn't like my little brother because every time she saw my little brother, it's like looking at herself in the mirror and not being happy with herself.

When my grandmother was growing up, her mother's mother treated her worse than a slave because of the color of her skin— her skin was dark. Now her brother was her grandmother's favorite because he was lighter than my grandmother. Her grandmother used to have her out in the cold chopping wood while her brother was in the house eating a hot meal. Her grandmother had a big house, and she rented out rooms. She said they would pay for renting a room, or they would pay for room and boarding. She said her grandmother would make her take the food to the people who was paying for room and board. She said about the time she carried their food and sat to eat, her food would be frozen cold and stiff like a brick. She said it would be so frozen if she were to throw the food at someone, it would knock them completely unconscious.

My grandmother said she was the black sheep of the family when she was growing up. It's sad to say that due to my grandmother being darker than her brother, she went through a lot of stuff. My grandmother's grandmother could not stand her own because of the color of her skin. My grandmother's brother Jonny, she worshiped the ground he walked on, but he would be the one who brought so many tears to his grandmother's eyes. My grandmother, who she hated and did not like, was the one who took care of her. She told my grandmother that she could not believe she was the one who was taking care of her, and my grandmother said, "For years, you treated me like shit and here is Jonny, your favorite, and he stops past and doesn't even come and say hello or just to see how you are doing."

My grandmother had to make Jonny go in there and say hello because her grandmother heard Jonny's voice and started to call him. He ignored her like he did not hear her She started to cry, and my grandmother went downstairs and told Jonny, if he didn't get his ass upstairs and say hello, she was going to whip his ass. Now Jonny did not play with my grandmother; she always used to kick Jonny's ass and fight Jonny's battle for him. He used to get his ass kicked because he could not fight, so he went upstairs and said hello. It was more than right because he brought a lot of tears to his grandmother's eyes and she helped raised him. Jonny was out there getting high. He stole from his grandmother and his sister, my grandmother, but was still my grandmother's grandmother's favorite, and she treated her granddaughter like shit because of the color of her skin, which was black just like hers, and that's who took care of her when she could no longer take care of herself.

I say this to people, treat all your loved ones with the same amount of love. There should not be a favorite. There should be equal love because the one you call your favorite may not be the one who takes care of you in the end; it may be the one who you could not stand for no reason, the one who you gave the most problems, the one who you treated like shit. It isn't always the one who you call your favorite that stays by your side a lot of time. It may be that person who you treated like shit whom you have to depend on, the one you would talk to like they are less than a person. You never know who God is going put in your corner when you need that person the most.

Now my grandmother became like her grandmother and here's why I say that. My mother was getting high heavily out here in these streets to the point she could not take care of me and my other brothers, so she asked my grandmother and her mother if they could take us so we would not go into a foster home. She brought us to my grandmother's house, and they picked us according to the color. Our grandmother's mother chose my brother Nathan because he was lighter than myself and my little brother, Moses. My grandmother chose me because I was lighter than Moses. They both looked at my little brother and was like they are not raising him because he was too dark, which is some fucked-up shit coming from two black women who are his grandmothers. You would think with all that my grandmother had been through with her mother's mother about the color of her skin, she would have wanted to raise my brother Moses. So my mother raised Moses because both of my grandmothers did not want to raise him due to the color of his skin. I don't understand to this day why my grandmother doesn't love my brother. She doesn't even claim none of his children as her grandchildren. She has become the woman who at one time she did not like, which was her grandmother. It's fucked that racism can go on with your family, with the people who have the same skin color as you and are your flesh and blood. My grandmother became her grandmother because my cousins who are a lighter skin tone—still black but just a lighter color—they are her favorite grandchildren, which is fucked up. My brother, still to this day, is trying to find out what he did or just wants to know why his grandmother doesn't show him the same love that she showed her other grandchildren.

I think when she sees my brother, it's like looking herself in the mirror, and everything that she hates about herself comes back to full surface. I think my grandmother went through a stage where she did like herself due to her grandmother and her family members who treated her like she was not even family. I would have rather lived in a foster home, then I would have more of an understanding on why I was treated less than family, but for my grandmother to be treated like that with her own flesh and blood, that's what makes that shit insane. I am pretty sure my grandmother wished she was in a foster home because maybe she would have been treated better. I think my grandmother built up some type of self-hate because of the color of her skin and the way she was treated due to it. She became a bully to her own grandson and his kids, which is a shame. I don't know, but it is still like that to this day. She had her favorites, who are much lighter than certain grandchildren.

After I was done talking to my grandmother on the phone, I told her I loved her and would talk to her later. I could not go back to sleep, so I just went and washed my face, brushed my teeth, fixed myself something to eat, went back upstairs and watched TV, and ate.

About two hours went by, and Tonya called my phone. She told me her and Chantelle were on their way back to the house. I said okay, so after I was done eating, I went downstairs and washed the dishes. I could hear the front door being unlocked. It was Tonya and Chantelle, so I went outside to get the bags of things for the party. I brought everything to the house then went back upstairs. Tonya and Chantelle were making the party bags and getting everything ready for Mama's party. I could hear the front door being unlocked. It was Ronald, Jamal, and Keith. Now Keith had told Ronald that he could get a drink from upstairs in me and Tonya's room, so he came upstairs and knocked on the door and said, "What up, Q? Keith said I could get a cup of liquor?"

So after Ronald got the liquor, he went back downstairs. Tonya called me. She asked me if I could go to the store.

I said, "Okay, what do you need?"

She said, "A pack of cigarettes and a Pepsi," so I went to the store.

By the time I got to the front door, I could hear Keith yelling at somebody, cursing that person out, so I opened the door. He was cussing Ronald out, saying, "I should beat your bitch ass up. I told you could get one cup of liquor and your bitch ass drank the whole bottle?"

That dude Ronald looked like he was scared as shit. He looked like he was guilty as well.

I said, "I was at the store that long, and this man done drunk a whole bottle of liquor?"

Tonya had to calm Keith down, and she told Ronald to get the fuck out the house, go take a walk before Keith put his hands on him. Ronald was just standing there with the dumb look on his face, so he left the house.

Mama's birthday party started at about 3:30, so I cooked hamburgers, hot dogs, and fried chicken. Somebody had cooked macaroni salad, potato salad. They had chips, juice. Someone made deviled eggs. All the kids ate, and they had a chance to knock the piñata open with the candy in it. None of the kids could break the piñata, so Jessie ended up breaking it for the kids, and they ended picking up the candy off the floor. Once that was over, everyone came and sang "Happy Birthday." Bryant was at the party. Mama's birthday party was a well-celebrated party.

Now Keith's birthday party would not be the same. Here's why I said that. The party started out okay. Tonya's homegirls came, and Jamal's people came. All Keith's Blood homeboys were at the party. There were a lot of Bloods there. Everybody was drinking and talking to whoever they were talking to. I was drinking as well. Now the front door was wide open because people were walking in and out the house. I went to walk out the front door, and Ronald was walking in the house, and this dude had the nerve to shoulder bump me. I said, "Watch where the fuck you are walking and say fucking 'excuse me.'"

This motherfucker went to say, "You're excused," as if I bumped into him. I threw a punch, and that's when I realized that I was feeling the liquor because I was falling as I was throwing the punch. I could hear people laughing. That shit made me mad, so I jumped right back up, and every punch I threw after that landed. I whipped his ass all the way from the front door to the back door, so I had about five to six people trying to pull me back to the front door, but they could not. It took Chantelle jumping in front of Ronald and crying. That's when I came back to reality because I was gone. You know how people say they lost it, or they snapped? Well, that was me.

So after I came back to reality I left out the front door, but that would not be the end of the ass whipping. Ronald had his people in the car waiting for him—his boyfriend and his family member. I was outside by the dumpster. I could hear Ronald leaving the house, and he was carrying two plates of food. When he got there by the dumpster, I smacked the shit out of him and was beating his ass to the point there was macaroni salad all over the ground. His boyfriend jumped out the car. I said, "What his bitch as going to do?"

He said, "I don't want any trouble. I am going to call the police."

The woman going to say, "Yeah, call the police. I said, "Bitch, mind your business."

She said she was going to call her boyfriend.

I said, "Bitch, call him." Damien was right there when she said she was going to call her boyfriend and his homeboy and they are going to jump me. Before I could say, "Bitch, call them again," Damien said, "Yeah, Ard bitch ain't nobody jumping Q."

So shorty said something to Damien, and Chantelle said, "Yeah, okay, ain't a motherfucking soul going to touch my little brother," and started making her way over there to shorty when Keith and Jessie pulled her back and calm her down.

Shorty said, "I am going to call the police," so they got in the car, including Ronald, and drove off, so me and Damien walked across the street to the basketball court because I could see the house from the basketball court. Damien was shooting around the basketball court. I was looking at the house and seeing if the police were pulling up. They did not call no police. At least no police ever came to the house that night, so me and Damien walked back over to the house.

Now a lot of people had left after the ass whipping. It was Chantelle Kevin, Keith, Jessie, and Mama who were still there, so Jessie asked Keith if he could drop her off at home. He said he would, so Keith said thanks to his mother and me for his birthday party.

We said, "You welcome."

Chantelle and Kevin were waiting on James to come pick them up, so after everybody left, me and Tonya went upstairs and went to sleep. The next day, when me and Tonya had woken up, Tonya received a phone call from her daughter Chantelle. She said, Jessie called her and told her that they had to take Ronald to the hospital. That's how bad Stepfather beat him."

Tonya said, "Damn!"

Now the next two months would get even crazier. That next month, which was September, was Bryant's birth month. September 9 was Bryant's birthday. He came over Tonya's house that night to get a couple of dollars from Tonya, but nobody in the house remembered that it was his birthday, so after he got what he came to get from Tonya and as he was going down the stairs to leave, he said, "Fuck all y'all. None of y'all even said happy birthday. Y'all did not remember my birthday," and left the house and slammed the door behind him. This would be the last time the last day that me and Tonya would see Bryant alive because that next month, Bryant would be killed. Now around the second week of October, me and Tonya had talked about getting life insurance because she had no life insurance on none of the kids; she did not have life insurance on herself too. My grandmother got life insurance on me when I was young, so my life insurance policy is paid in full.

I was like, "Baby, you don't have life insurance on none of your children, and they are grown now."

She said she had life insurance on the children, but she stopped paying the insurance payments

I said, "Damn, baby," so we got all the paperwork together and filled out the papers. We were going to make our first payments the end of the month of October. Here's why it is important to get some type of life insurance because the end of the month of October, we were going to start making our first payments on the life insurance policy when Bryant got killed. I would never forget that day. When Tonya got that phone call, she was in the room standing on the bed, putting something on the wall. I had stepped out the room into the hallway when I heard her cell phone ring. I heard her answer the phone and say, "Hello?"

The next sound I heard was a chilling scream.

"No, no, no, no, no!" I rushed my ass back in to the room. Tonya had dropped on the bed, and she was crying real loud. She said, "They killed Bryant. They killed Bryant!"

It was chilling because I could see and feel her pain. She handed me the phone, and the person who was on the other end said they took him to Johns Hopkins Hospital. I got off the phone, and I grabbed Tonya and hugged her.

I said, "I am sorry, baby," and she continued to cry in my arms. "Baby, I am here for you, and we are going to get through this together, but you got to bring it together." I told her how much I loved her.

Jamal was there. He came in the room and said, "Ma, it's going to be okay" and gave her a hug. He told her how much he loved her. Tonya had calmed down a little. Her phone kept ringing, people calling about Bryant, so me and Tonya got dressed. Keith was coming to pick us up and drive us to the hospital. Jamal and Damien went to the hospital as well, so when we arrived at the hospital, Jessie was there. Bryant's godmother and her children were there.

Tonya walked up to the room where they had Bryant at, and you could see what was in the room through the door window. When Tonya walked up to the door and looked in the room, she lost it. She started screaming and crying. I walked over to the door and looked. The way they had Bryant laid out on the table dead, that shit pissed me the fuck off. It's like they tried to revive him, and when they could not revive him, they just left him there, just left him on the table dead, so I walked over there to Tonya. She was hugging Bryant's godsister. I started rubbing Tonya's back. She said she needed some air, so we left the hospital and sat in front of the hospital. I was holding Tonya. She said Chantelle was on her way down there as well as her mother and father. Her sister was on her way too, so Chantelle and Kevin and Nate got there first. Chantelle was going through it. She came and hugged her mother, and she was crying.

After Chantelle and Tonya had calmed down, we all sat in front of the hospital, then Mother Tones and Father Tones pulled up. They came and set next to Tonya and gave her a hug. Then Tonya's sister Lora pulled up and gave Tonya and her mother a hug. We sat in front of the hospital until it got dark.

Lora and Tonya were talking about funeral arrangements. Mother Tones and Father Tones had gone home, and Lora told Tonya to call her tomorrow so they could go over the funeral arrangements, then she went home now. After we were done at the hospital, we did not go home. We went to the block where Bryant was killed, which was 2500 Hoffman Street, right there next to the store, Jimmy's carry-out. Now Jimmy's sat right on the corner of Hoffman. You got houses right next to Jimmy's like row homes. Bryant was killed on the stairs of the second house from the corner of Jimmy's. He was killed in broad daylight.

When we got on Hoffman Street, there was still blood on the steps where Bryant was killed, and the people who were living there at that time, they had a screen door that was black, with glass and bars. All the glass and the screen was shattered. There was about twenty people out there. There were candles out there, so we sat on the steps of the house and took a picture. Now Bryant's godbrothers were out there as well, so we sat on the steps and took a picture. It was not a picture of celebrating. It was not a picture of smiles. You could tell everybody in the picture was angry and pissed off, so we stayed out there for about an hour, and after we were done, we got in the car now.

On the way home, Keith was telling the story of what he heard happened to Bryant. He said word on the street was it was retaliation 'cause Bryant had killed their people, so they came and got revenge for their people. He said that two people came up to Bryant. One person was on a bike, and the other person was walking next to the person who was on the bike. They got close to Bryant and said, "What up, Bryant?" and the person who was on the bike gave Bryant a five, which means a handshake, and then pulled the gun out and shot Bryant till the gun was empty, then him and the person who walked up to Bryant left the area on the bike.

Keith dropped us off at the house. When we got in the house, everybody was quiet. Damien went in his room. Jamal went in his room. I asked Tonya what she wanted to eat because she had not eaten all day. She said she was not hungry. There is no pain more hurtful in this world than a parent having to bury their child. Tonya went through that twice. She had lost her first son, baby Tyler, at the age of two or three. His godmother and godfather killed him by pouring gasoline on him and lighted him on fire. I cannot even imagine. If I had known Tonya at this time, the godmother and godfather would not have made it to a court date. They would have been six feet under. You are sick individuals—cold individuals—to kill a baby, to rape a child or woman, to harm a child in any way. I say punishment should be death. You are messed up individuals to harm a child or woman. You are cowards. The crazy thing is, both the godmother and godfather were released from prison after doing something so horrendous. She had to endure that pain twice. I could not say to her, "Baby, I know what you are going through," because I have not gone through that, but I did say to her, "Baby, I am hurting because you are hurting. We are going through this together. Bryant was my family too, baby. I am in your corner through everything, baby."

She said she could not believe what happened. She started crying. I wiped the tears from her face and kissed her on her cheeks and told her I loved her. Baby, it's going to get better. We just got to take one day at a time," so Tonya ended up falling asleep. I ended up falling asleep myself.

The next day, me and Tonya woke and called around to see if we could get the city to help bury Bryant. This is why it is important to get some type of insurance on you and your loved ones because we never know when God is going to call us home; it is important to get insurance so your people won't to have to run all around or call around the city trying to scrape up some money to give your people a proper burial. This is why a lot of people get cremated. While they are here on earth, they are not worrying about getting life insurance, or their parents were not worrying about getting life insurance; they feel like they have enough time to get one. Only God knows the amount of time we have here on earth, so it is good to invest in insurance to leave your loved ones stress-free and not having to figure out where are they going to get the money to give you the proper burial, but me and Tonya would have to go through this the hard way with her not having any insurance on Bryant; the city would not be able to help us. So she called Bryant father and asked if he had any money to contribute to the funeral of his son. Now Bryant's father did not live in Baltimore. He lived out of state. He said not only did he have no money to contribute to his son's funeral, he would not be attending his funeral. Now that some cold-blooded shit. How do you help make a child and not want anything to do with your child? Even when your child passes away, you still don't want nothing to do with him. You are a fucked-up person.

So after Tonya got off the phone with Bryant's father, she called Lora. Lora asked if she had any type of life insurance on Bryant. She said no. She asked if she would be able to scrape up some money from somewhere. Tonya said no, so Lora said, "Tonya, this is why it is important to have life insurance, so you won't have to scrape up money to get to pay for funeral." Lora told Tonya that she would borrow $2,000. She told Tonya that the money would have to be paid back as soon as possible, plus she said she would call around to see if she could scrape up some more money for the funeral because $2,000 won't even pay for a casket, which is true. Nowadays you need at least a $10,000 life insurance policy just to cover a funeral. It has become very expensive over the years just to bury your loved ones, so after Tonya got off the phone, she called around to family members, but nobody had anything to contribute.

Now that night they were giving a candlelight vigil for Bryant. Tonya did not want to go, but Jessie came to the room and was like, "Auntie, we are going to this candlelight vigil for Bryant," so we all went. Me, Tonya, Damien, and Jessie got in the car with Keith. He drove to the candlelight. Jamal and Ronald got in the car with one of Jamal's homeboys.

When we got to the candlelight vigil, there was a lot of people out there, and they had a lot of lit candles arranged in an order that spelled out "RIP, Maniac," which was one of Bryant's nickname. They had balloons tied to the sidewalk pole. They had teddy bears right next to the candles. There was a lot of people who came out and showed Bryant love the night of the candlelight vigil.

Jessie started screaming out, "This has to stop! We are killing each other for nothing. This has got to stop. They have taken my cousin away from his family…" She broke down crying.

The newspeople were out there, and they wanted to know if the mother of the victim was out. They asked would she mind saying anything to the camera? So Tonya and Jamal spoke on the news camera. I forgot what they said, but it made the news though. I noticed the police was out there, parked across the street like they were waiting for something to happen. We stayed at the candlelight vigil for about an hour and a half, then we got back in the car, and Keith drove me, Tonya, Jessie, and Damien home.

When we got to the house, I went upstairs. Tonya stayed downstairs talking to Jessie, Keith, Jamal, and Ronald. Damien went in his room and watched TV.

The next day would get crazy. Tonya would find out that Bryant's godmother, who she does not like, had a life insurance policy and was trying to get a copy of Bryant's death certificate, which is crazy. This lady really thought she was Bryant's biological mother, and what's crazy is if she could have gotten her hands on Bryant's death certificate, she was going to get that life insurance money and was planning not to spend a dime of that money on Bryant's funeral, which would have been fucked up, to say the least. This is somebody you supposedly loved and called your godson. She was trying to use Bryant's death as a payday, but she realized that she could not use the life insurance policy if she did not have that death certificate, and the person who had the death certificate was Bryant's biological mother, Tonya. I would have liked to see her face when they told her she could not use the life insurance without the death certificate. They also probably asked her, "Are you the biological parent?"

So Tonya called Lora and told her the news, so Lora was like, "Hell no, she got a life insurance policy and she did say anything thing about it?" I don't know what big sister Lora said to Bryant's godmother, but the next day, it was Tonya and Lora and Bryant's godmother on the phone, talking about the life insurance. The godmother agreed that she would put up some money from the life insurance policy, which was more than right, so they agreed to meet up in person, all three of them, to go over arranging Bryant's funeral the next day. They said they would come over Tonya's house to discuss everything.

The next day I heard Lora say, "We are adults. You all need to squash whatever issues you all have with each other," so everything was set for the next day. I don't know what Lora said to get Tonya and Bryant's godmother on the phone, but she did know Lora was a beautiful strong black woman who had no cut cards. She was straightforward; she was not going to sugarcoat anything. She was going to tell you how it was, and if she could help you, she would. She didn't mind helping anyone if she could. Her and Tonya were not close. If you did not know them, you would not have thought they were sisters because they are distant, and Tonya played a major role in why they were not close. Lora tried to get closer to her sister, but I think Tonya could not take Lora's brutal honesty 'cause Lora was going to tell you when you were wrong, and Tonya was spoiled rotten. This is my opinion, but Tonya was the reason she did not want to get close with her sister. Tonya was the youngest out her sisters. Lora was the second oldest, and they had an older sister who passed away, which was Jessie and her brother's mother.

So the next day, Lora, Tonya, and Bryant's godmother were sitting in the dining room table discussing where the viewing was going to be, where the funeral was going to be at, as well as where Bryant was going to be buried. They were going over what day they should have the viewing in the funeral. After they went over everything, they agreed on everything, so the next day they would go to the funeral home and go over the price of everything. Tonya agreed to give Bryant's godmother a copy of the death certificate so she could get the money from the life insurance policy and put up some money toward the funeral.

The next day, we ended up going to the funeral place. Tonya, Lora, and Bryant's godmother talked to the person who owned the funeral home. They went over everything like the cost for the casket, and they got everything in order. They decided that they would have Bryant's viewing at that place, but they decided to have his funeral at another place located on Belair Road. So the viewing of Bryant was on Wednesday, and the funeral was that Thursday so that next week was a crazy week starting at Bryant's viewing. They had two viewing times for Bryant. The first time was in the afternoon, the second time was in the evening. Now the place where they had the viewing was something because it was a house. It's like the funeral director who owned the house said, "I am going to make the house a funeral home," and that's what he did. It was a row house that was turned into a funeral home. Inside, there was not that much space. That's one of the reasons they just decided to have the viewing there.

Me, Tonya, Keith, Damien, Jamal, Ronald, Chantelle, and Jessie, we all went to the viewing that was in the evening. Lora and Mother Tones and Father Tones met us at the funeral home. It was about 4:00 p.m. when we got there. Now when we got to the viewing, there were a lot of people there. A lot of people came out and paid their respects they had Bryant in the casket. You could see where he had been shot, where they tried to cover the bullet wounds up. They did the best they could, but Bryant had been shot in his face. You could still see it. He was shot in his hand, and the bullet came out his hand and went in his face. When they got to shooting him, he tried to cover up, and that's how the bullet exited his hand and entered his face. Everybody just was standing, crying, watching Bryant.

Tonya walked up to the casket and stood over Bryant, and she told him that she loved him. Bryant was only eighteen when he got killed. That's how it is in my city. You are blessed if you make it to twenty-five because brothers are getting killed before then.

Now Tonya had gone and sat down. I went and sat down next to her. People who came to pay their respects would come up to Tonya and give her a hug and say, "Sorry for your loss."

Now Bryant's godmother came in from outside, and she said Tenon was their now. Tenon was Tonya's ex-boyfriend. When she said that, she was looking at me the whole time, so I guess she thought that it would bother me. That shit did not bother me. I knew Tonya was my woman, but an insecure brother would have a problem with him being there, so I went outside the funeral home, and I saw the dude Tenon and Keith and one of Bryant's godbrothers. They were looking at Keith's phone. I would later find out that they were showing Keith a picture of the man who killed his brother. You could hear the dude Tenon say, "I told Bryant to leave the corner that day." He said he pulled up on Bryant and told him he needed to lie low after what he just did. He said Bryant was hard-headed; he would not listen. He said shortly after he pulled off, Bryant was killed. He said if Bryant had left off them stairs and left from the area, he would still be alive, so after they were done talking, this dude Tenon, he gave me a look like, "Man, yeah, I know who you are," like he wanted to fight. I gave the same stare back like, "What's up, dude? I don't fear, nobody but God," so that man ended up walking back up the street. I went back into to the funeral home and sat back beside Tonya. She whispered in my ear, "Baby, I did not know he would be here."

I said, "Baby, it's no problem." Satan was busy that day, but Satan is a liar, so Tonya and Bryant's godmother got into an argument. I forgot what it was over, but Lora got everything in order on some grow woman shit, so after we were done at the viewing, we all went home. A little later that night, me and Tonya got into an argument over some petty shit. It was so petty I don't even remember what we were arguing over, but it was one of them arguments where both of us said some shit. It was to the point where the next day I was not going to the funeral. That's how mad I was.

So the next day, they were getting ready to go to the funeral, and I was not getting dressed. I know I was being petty at that time, so Ronald came and talked to me. He said, "Q, I am not getting in y'all's business. I know both of y'all are upset with each other right now."

He said, "But, Q, Tonya is going to need you by her side to help her get through this. You all love each other 'cause you all have been through a lot and you are going through a lot, but you all are still together. Today, Q, Tonya is going to need you more than ever. She is about to bury her son, and before he died, they were not on good terms. This is the second time she had to go through this pain."

Now I had to admit everything Ronald was saying was right, so after Ronald was done talking, he left the room, and me and Tonya started talking. I told her I loved her and that I was going to the funeral. Now me and Tonya got dressed. Now after we got ourselves together, the limo was out front. We all got into the limousine, and it took all of us to the funeral.

When we got to the funeral and went inside, there were a lot of people. The funeral had not even started yet. About time the funeral did start, there were even more people. There were so many that people had to stand up; there was no room to sit down. Now Bryant did a lot of wrong, but he had a lot of love from everybody who showed up at that funeral. He had teachers who came out and paid their respects.

The pastor being speaking. While he was speaking, Bryant's godsister was standing over his casket. She was so close everybody thought she was going to climb in the casket with Bryant. That's how close she was to the casket, which was crazy because when Bryant was alive, she did not like him or give a damn about him, and he did not like her or give a damn about her.

There was a seat next to me and Tonya, so Kevin sat down. He said, "What up, Q?" He was shedding tears. The pastor asked if anyone had any words they would like to say, so one of Bryant's teachers got up there. She said Bryant was a very intelligent young man. She said he was a straight A student. She said Bryant wanted to open up a center that would help prevent children from going on the corner or breaking laws, a place where they could come get help with their homework, play sports, a place where they could get a meal because a lot of children in our city's households are from families that may be struggling, that may not be able to provide a meal to their children. Bryant wanted to change that by opening up the recreational centers for the kids to have a place that was positive to go after school, where they could get help with their homework, get another meal, and have a good time by playing games and sports. Bryant was planning to give back to the youth with something positive so they would not end up doing something negative like going to the streets and committing crimes such as robbing people, selling drugs. Bryant wanted to open up other options that were positive for the youth, but his life was cut short. After the teacher got done speaking on behalf of Bryant, a couple other people got up there and spoke about the time they spent with Bryant, and then Keith got up there. He was crying, and he said, "Bryant was my brother" real loud. "Whoever killed my brother, I am going to fucking kill him. I am going to fucking kill him!" He was shouting while Jessie and Jamal's people went up there to get him off the stage. Lora, Tonya's sister, got up there and spoke, and when she got up there, you could hear the pain in her voice to the point Tonya started crying. I wiped the tears from her eyes and then I started shedding tears myself. After everyone who wanted to say a few words for Bryant was done, the pastor said some more words on behalf of Bryant, then he let everybody know where the burial site would be. He said, "Will the pallbearers begin to push the casket of Bryant to the front door, so he can be put in the hearse?" So me and Keith pushed Bryant to the door of the funeral room home.

When we got to the front door, we looked out the door. There was a lot of water. One of the main water pipes had busted open, and it was right there next to the church. Water everywhere, so when they opened the door, the water came up to our knees. A couple of other people came to help carry the casket and put it in the hearse, so after we put the casket in the hearse, my shoes were soaking wet as well as my pants up to my knees, so me, Tonya, Bryant's godmother, Jamal, and Damien got in the limousine. We rode to the burial site. Everyone else got a ride or drove there. The drive was very awkward because it was quiet, and people were on their phone or looking out the window. When we got to the burial site, I got out the car, and we got the casket out the hearse. We walked him to the burial ground and sat the casket on the stand. Everybody said their goodbyes to Bryant. We stayed there for about an hour and a half, then me, Tonya, and her immediate family, we went back to the house. Bryant's godmother and her family went their way, along with everybody else that was not immediate family.

When we got back home, we all went in. The house was crowded, and at that time, me and Tonya did not have any furniture, so a lot of people were standing, and Mother Tones said something that I would never forget. She said, "Young man, where is your furniture at?" She did not say it loud. She called me over there and said, "You all need to get some furniture."

I said, "Mother Tones, I am about to get furniture for the living room and upstairs."

She said okay, so I went out the back door. Keith, Kevin, James, and Damien were outside. Keith was like, "Man, the dude who killed my brother, I am going to kill him."

I said, "When you ready to take care of that issue, we can go take care of it together. You know who done the shooting, that's a plus." I said when we do go take care the issue, he would have to change the car, get a rental car, gloves, face mask, and two guns, which I already had. He said okay. I said he got to do his homework and get some more information on the dude who shot Bryant. He said already he's going to do his homework, so after we got done talking, I went back into the house and went upstairs. It smelled like weed. They were smoking in me and Tonya's room, so I went in Damien's room and played NBA 2K.

After everybody left, I went downstairs to check up on Tonya and made sure she was good. She wanted me to fix her something to eat, so I fixed dinner for the whole house. Now that next week I would get a phone call from my lawyer saying that the city sent a check for me, $6,500, for selling my house that I owned. Plus I would get my federal taxes back, which was 5,000, so I had 11,500. So I went to my lawyer's office and picked up my check. My lawyer had already got his money off top, so the remaining money was mine, so after I left my lawyer's office, I went to my bank, which at that time was Bank of America. When I got there, it was a little crowded, so I waited in the line. When I got to the front, I told the teller I wanted to deposit this check into my bank account. She asked for my bank card. I gave her my card. She asked me if I wanted to open up a savings account.

I said, "No, I am good."

She said about $1,800 of the money would be available that day, and the rest of the money would be on the card the next day, so I said, "Okay, thank you. Have a nice day."

She said, "You do the same," so I left the bank, and I called Tonya and told her that I'd gotten the check and deposited it in my bank. I said, "I am going to pay Lora a thousand so she can pay whoever she borrowed the money from to help bury Bryant." Keith was paying the other half of the money, another thousand dollars. I said, "We are going to get a living room set."

She said, "You want to go get the furniture today?"

I said, "We can go get the furniture." So after I was done at the bank, I went home. Christmas was right around the corner, so when I got back home, I called my mother and told her I would have some money for her as well as my grandmother. I called my baby mother as well. I told her that I would be to pick up Kiwi on Saturday. I also told her about my check for my house. I said, "I am about to go crazy for Kiwi this Christmas." I asked if she needed anything. She said no, she was good. I said I would get Kayla and Hayden, Kiwi's older sister and brother, some shoes. She said, "Thanks."

I said, "No problem." I talked to my daughter, and I told her I loved her and would be there Saturday to pick her up. When I got off the phone, I went talk to Damien. I said, "Damien, since you been doing good in school, what do you want for Christmas?"

He said, "An iPad, two pairs of Nike Foamposites, a new TV."

I said, "I am going to buy a new box spring and mattress as well as a dresser. The dog used to piss in this bed. It's time for everything new in this house."

He said he wanted a futon bunk bed.

I said, "Well, go on Walmart and find the bunk bed you want, and I am going to pay for it," so he went on Walmart and found a futon bunk bed, so I ordered the bunk bed as well as three TVs. I believe when God blesses you with something, that blessing is not just for you. God blesses you for you to be a blessing for someone else. That's what I did. I made sure everybody was good. I got everything my daughter wanted for Christmas. I gave my mother money. I gave Tonya, Chantelle, and Keith money as well as Jamal. I bought Tonya some pocketbooks. I also bought what Damien asked for Christmas. I gave Lora the money back that she borrowed to help bury Bryant. I gave my uncle money. I gave my cousins money. I gave my grandmother money. I bought furniture for the house. I brought me and Tonya a whole new bedroom set, a queen pillow top box spring and mattress, headboard, footboard, two nightstands, and a dresser. Tonya wanted a little vanity where she could sit and put her makeup on. I felt good being able to look out for my family as well as put smiles on their faces. It made me thank God for blessing me to be able to be a blessing to my family. Little did I know that the last months of that year and the following year would get even crazier. I would get locked up, and I would lose five years of my daughter's life.

Stay tuned for part 2 of this book. Thank you all for taking out the time to read this book. May God bless you all. I want to thank God for allowing me to stay focused on finishing this first book, for giving me the patience to not give up. I want to send a special shout-out to Mother Jones. May she rest in peace. I want to send a shout-out to Donna. May she rest in peace as well.

I want to send a shout-out to my grandmother. May she rest in peace. May Donnell rest in peace as well. I love you all, and until I see you all again, RIP, may you all be safe and God bless.

A LETTER TO MY GRANDMOTHER

Our grandmother was a strong black queen who loved her children and grandchildren. She was selfless, meaning she sacrificed a lot to provide for her family. One of the ways she sacrificed was by raising her grandchildren. If it had not been for my grandmother stepping in and showing selflessness, I would have been in a foster home. They said it takes a village to raise a child. I say no, all you need is an extraordinary and amazing grandmother like ours. I put my grandmother through a lot of ups and downs, but she never gave up on me. She was always there. Grandma always said, "As family, we got to stick together no matter what."

I have a lot of great memories with Grandma that I will never forget. Even though you have gone to your next journey in life, Ma, you will not be forgotten. I would not be the man I am today if it had not been for my grandmother and all the values and principles she taught me. One of the memories I share with my grandmother is going to the store and getting her scratch-off lottery tickets. I got them wrong, and Grams was so upset with me. I think everybody in the family had this same problem. You better bring back the correct lottery ticket as well as scratch-offs, or else you were going to hear it from Grams. You never know how much you love a person until they are no longer there and you can't talk to them no more or see them no more, then you realize how much they meant to you and how meaningful they were to your life. Grams was the glue that held the family together. I just thank God for blessing me with the time and the moments me and Grams shared. I wouldn't change anything, Ma. Until we see you again. We love you as well as miss you. We truly appreciated everything you have done as well as the unconditional love you had for all of us. May you rest in peace.

ABOUT THE AUTHOR

Quintin Ford is a God-fearing man who is also a loving husband as well as a loving father as well as a son he is a family man who is a hard worker who is loyal he will give you the shirt off his back as well as shoes off his feet if I had to use one word to describe Quintin Ford is selfless he put the wants in needs of other before his own wants in needs he was born in the rugged city of Baltimore which is also known as body more murda land if you know you know where every day is a struggle just to stay above the ground Quintin Truly believes that as long you have god by your side there is no obstacle you cannot overcome you just got work hard for whatever it is that you may be trying to achieve in God will see the hard work and dedication you are putting in, God will make sure you succeed you just got believe in see your vision when nobody else see it.

www.ingramcontent.com/pod-product-compliance
Lightning Source LLC
Chambersburg PA
CBHW021205130726
47988CB00002B/521